BLACKFOOT CRAFT BOOK

Compiled by Adolf and Beverly Hungry Wolf

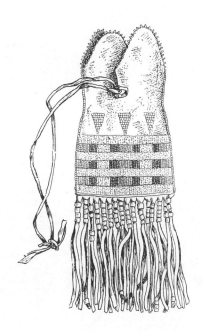

BOOK PUBLISHING COMPANY
SUMMERTOWN, TENNESSEE
USA

GOOD MEDICINE BOOKS
SKOOKUMCHUCK, B.C.
CANADA

ISBN 0-913990-80-9

Book Publishing Company
PO Box 99
Summertown, TN 38483

Good Medicine Books
Box 844
Skookumchuck, BC
Canada V0B 2E0

Copyright © 1977 by Adolf Hungry Wolf
Revised Edition 1983
Revised Edition, second printing 1991
Revised Edition, third printing 1993

Hungry Wolf, Adolf.
　　　Blackfoot craftworker's book / compiled by Adolf and Beverly Hungry Wolf. — Rev. ed.
　　　　　　　p. cm.
　　　Rev. ed. of: Blackfoot craftworker's book. c1977.
　　　Includes bibliographical references (p. 80).
　　　ISBN 0-913990-80-9 : $11.95
1. Siksika Indians—Industries. 2. Siksika Indians—Costume and adornment. 3. Handicraft—British Columbia. I. Hungry Wolf, Beverly. II. Hungry Wolf, Adolf. Blackfoot craftworker's book. III. Title.
E99.S54H86 1983
745.5'089'973—dc20　　　　　　　　　　　　　　　91-18003
　　　　　　　　　　　　　　　　　　　　　　　　　　　CIP

Table of Contents

Acknowledgements

The following Persons and institutions helped us to learn ways of traditional Blackfoot craftwork and to do research into the technical aspects of the subject. If we had cared to do more travelling and researching this list would no doubt be longer. It seems like Blackfoot articles form a part of every museum collection that deals very much with North American tribes. Though the ones we have seen are only a few, they are certainly the major ones concerning the tribes of the Blackfoot Nation. The locations of articles in this book are identified by museum initials, which are explained below. Our thanks to the following:

Willie Eagle Plume; Ruth Little Bear; Paula Weasel Head; Annie Red Crow; and Joseph Young Eagle Child, for teaching us.

Nora Spanish and Louise Evans of the Blackfeet Craft Shop, St. Mary, Montana.

John Ewers and Clark Wissler for their past anthropological researching.

Eric Waterton, of the Provincial Museum and Archives of Alberta (PMAA), Edmonton, Alberta.

Dr. Stanley Freed, of the American Museum of Natural History (AMNH), New York City.

U. Vincent Wilcox III, of the Museum of the American Indian, Heye Foundation (Heye), New York.

Ramon Ganje and Loretta Pepion, of the Museum of the Plains Indian (MPI), Browning, Montana.

Wendy Rose, of the Lowie Museum (LM), University of California, Berkeley.

Introduction

The main purpose of this book is to encourage craftworkers among the divisions of the Blackfoot Nation to learn the traditional styles of their own People's culture. The articles illustrated in here are in the collections of various museums throughout North America. Most of them are not readily accessible to Blackfoot craftworkers. Many of them are stored in dark rooms, surrounded by the smell of mothballs. Museums have only limited display space, and generally select only the finest articles to keep out. This book, then, is your own personal version of a museum display on the Blackfoot material culture.

In recent years there has been a revival of interest in traditional ways and materials, especially among the younger generations. At tribal dances and pow-wows one can see results of this revival by looking around at the many "old-time-styled-outfits" worn by participants. From conversations we have heard, it looks like this revival will continue to grow in the times ahead. Yet, there are very few craftworkers who know the traditional styles well enough to create them or teach them to others. Particularly lacking among the People, by this time in history, are many examples of old craftwork that might inspire new variations. Such articles have been eagerly bought, for many years now, by museums and private collectors, when they were not lost or buried with their last owners. Makers and users of traditional craftwork will do well if they can discipline themselves not to be tempted into giving up their articles for large sums of money. The articles can provide many lifetimes of pride and pleasure, both for their original owners as well as for those who may inherit them as treasures of their ancestry. The money that these articles bring, when sold, seldom brings more than momentary satisfaction.

This collection of photographs was not begun with the intention of turning into a book. It has served, for many years, as a reference source for my own family's efforts to learn the traditional craftwork of our Native relations of the Past. This craftwork has been a visual part of our devotion to Blackfoot traditions as our way of family life. It is up to each of you to decide how much of your life you wish to devote to traditions already tried and proven successful, and how much you want to devote to new, modern ways. This book is not meant to advocate a "return to the Old Ways," though it will sure help, if that's what you intend to try to do.

Because many of these photographs were taken only to serve as references for our family, their quality is often far from "professional." Hopefully, only "professionals" will notice this, to any extent. If they are not satisfied, they may wish to go and take similar photos of their own, with better cameras and equipment. We have generally used a single-lens, 35 millimeter camera, without tripod, flash, or fancy accessories. We took the photos by whatever lighting was in the rooms where we worked. In some cases this meant one bare 100-watt light bulb--not the best for making nice pictures. We used Black-and-White film, because it was cheap and easy. Colored pictures would be beautiful to have, since all the work was originally made with many colors. The fact is, we couldn't afford colored film at the time, and we couldn't afford to make this book with colored pictures, now. Colored books cost a great deal more to produce than black and white ones. Use your skill and imagination at creating pleasant color combinations.

One season of work on this book was carried out with the help of an Explorations Grant from the Canada Council. During this period we worked on the project with our Family Elder, Willie Eagle Plume (Atsitsina, or Prairie Owl Man), a noted ceremonial leader and craftworker among the Bloods. We intended to go through this photo collection and create one example of each kind of article--listing the materials used (including their sources and costs), describing the history and methods, and illustrating the actual construction work. The result would have been much more of a "how-to" book than this is--sort of a <u>Foxfire Book</u> of the Blackfoot Nation, if you can imagine that. The project went along very slowly, since the old man was much more concerned with teaching us his ceremonial knowledge than his skills with crafts. He passed away in the Spring of 1976, long before the project was completed. We know of no one to take his place. So, the challenge remains with <u>you</u>, the craftworker, to learn the best methods of making traditional articles, after carefully studying the illustrations. We have had success doing this, ourselves.

History of Craftwork

All of the articles illustrated in this book were made after the "primitve days" of the long-ago. We don't really know much about the crafts made by the ancient Blackfoot People, though we can assume that they were pretty plain and basic. They were all made with materials found directly in Nature--hides, bones, woods, and so forth. More modern tools were eagerly sought by trade, from other tribes, even before the first traders ever came to the Blackfoot country. Try making a pair of moccasins with only a stone knife, a bone awl, and strands of sinew, and you will quickly see how those long-ago ancestors appreciated steel knives, scissors, and other tools.

Dr. Wissler gives a lot of information about the developments of various articles of craftwork in his volume on "Material Culture." Some of this information will interest modern craftworkers, but much of it is of little use in actually learning to make the crafts. The general summary of such a study is the most important point for modern craftworkers: Native craftworkers have always been influenced by the styles and ways of other Peoples (both Native and non-Native), and they have always made use of whatever tools and supplies they could get that made their work easier and better.

We don't know for sure that all the articles in this book were made by Blackfoot craftworkers. Museum records are often vague and sometimes noticeably wrong. Trading craftwork with other tribes has always been popular. One thing we can say, with certainty, is that all the articles in this book are of the style made and used in the Blackfoot Nation. A more important point, however, is that these illustrated articles were often the finest ones among the People, at the time they were obtained. Museum buyers and private collectors have usually sought the best decorated and most colorful articles, rather than the plain, well-worn, everyday ones. This is especially true with clothing. Don't let the examples make you think that the Old People always went around in beaded suits and dresses. Most People owned such fine clothing, but they kept it carefully packed away in their parfleche "suitcases" most of the time.

Styles and decorations of articles made by Blackfoot craftworkers were often quite similar to those made and used among neighboring tribes, although little details often separate one from the others. Crow, Cree, Kootenai, and Flathead crafts and styles are regularly confused with those from the Blackfoot Nation. In some cases, articles made by the Sarsi and Gros Ventre are identical, since these two tribes were often Blackfoot allies.

The photograph below shows Curly Bear, head chief of the South Piegans, with his remaining wife, Surrendering Woman, seated by some of their valued possessions, in 1912. These are examples of Blackfoot craftwork.

Clothing

Most of the clothing illustrated in this book was only worn on special occasions. It is not the traditional wear for everyday use. This is fortunate now, since traditional dress would only be used in parades, dances, and other celebrations. Even if we knew much about the everyday styles of the Past, there would be very little use for it, today.

The robe was the single most important article of dress in Blackfoot traditions. Even now it is acceptable to go on the dance grounds with only a blanket draped over an arm (for men) or a shawl over the shoulders (for women). Of course, this is with modern clothing underneath, though boys and men often wore nothing but a robe, way back in the Old Days. An old-time robe was usually from the hide of a Buffalo cow, softly tanned, with the hair left on. Out on the trail with nothing but such a robe, a man could wrap himself up in it and lay down for a warm sleep, or drop it off instantly in hot weather or at meeting some emergency. It is said that men in those days often raced into battle naked, after they had dropped their robes.

Summer robes were sometimes made from tanned Elk hides with the hair removed. All kinds of hide robes were often decorated with painted designs or embroidered quillwork. The robes of chiefs were sometimes covered with brilliant Sunbursts of red and yellow Porcupine quills. Warriors sometimes covered their robes with pictographic records of their noted exploits. Holy Men sometimes drew out their sacred visions and symbols. Most commonly, robes were decorated with parallel stripes and borders. Children were given tanned robes of Buffalo calf skins. Often they were sent out naked, to make them tough and to save their clothing.

Beef hides did not replace Buffalo as robes. Instead, the People turned to wool blankets given out by the government, or obtained in trade. Those with bright designs were preferred, along with the several brands that had stripes, like those offered by the Hudson's Bay Company. Elk hide robes show in photos of dances as late as the 1920's. They are still a part of the Holy Woman's outfit at times of the Sun Dance ceremonies.

Fringing was the main style of decoration on everyday hide clothing of the past. The hides were often smoked, to make them more durable and water-resistant. Hide clothing made for dress-up wear was not usually smoked, but often heavily decorated beyond fringing. The older styles of clothing tended to follow the natural styles of the hides, while the most modern styles are very tailored in appearance. This makes them look more "neat," but less flowing.

Moccasins

Two styles of moccasins are known in Blackfoot traditions, though only one of these is used today. The older style has a top and bottom made from one piece of soft hide, folded in half and sewn up on one side. Many generations knew this as the "Real Moccasin." It is soft and comfortable, but wears out quickly and is hard to repair. It is the style of moccasin used by many tribes on the West side of the Rocky Mountains.

According to the studies of John Ewers, Blackfoot craftworkers began making today's common two-piece style of moccasin in the early or middle nineteenth century. This style has a soft upper piece sewn to a hard sole, with stitches all the way around. It is the style of moccasin used by many tribes on the Plains, to the East.

With these two basic styles of moccasins, many variations are possible. Material, decorations, and ankle heights are the most important. These variations depend on what is available and what the moccasins will be used for. Of course, the easiest kind of moccasins to make are plain, low ones for everyday wear.

The members of our own family have been wearing nothing but moccasins for a number of years, now. Our favorite combination is the two-piece style, made with smoked Deerskin tops, latigo soles, and high ankle flaps. Rawhide soles were used in the Past, of course, but they are not so common, now. White hide for tops is often preferred, but this makes the moccasins harder to keep clean and, worst of all, subject to destruction if they get very wet. Although Elk and Moose hides are thicker and warmer than those of Deer, we found them to wear out much more quickly. After using many pairs of the old one-piece style moccasin, we have given it up as too costly. When the sole wears out, it cannot be replaced like one on a two-piece style. We use the one-piece style now only for Winter moccasins, which we make with Sheepskin, leaving the hair inside. Buffalo skin was used for the same purpose in the Old Days.

One begins to make either style of moccasin by cutting out a paper pattern based on a tracing of the wearer's foot. The tongues can be cut right into the tops, as shown in the sketches, or they can be added separately. In that case, the opening on top is cut in the form of a T. The paper pattern is then tried on the foot, and adjustments are made. Then the hide is cut according to the pattern. Moccasins are always sewn up inside out, to help hide and protect the stitches. Sewing on a one-piece moccasin begins on the short side and goes around to the back, then up, and finally across the small tab at the bottom. With the two-piece style the sewing begins at the toes and goes to the back, first around one side, then the other. A successful pattern is carefully saved for future use.

The completed one-piece style moccasin is too low to be practical, without the addition of ankle flaps. In Summer these might be only an inch or two high, but generally they were made to cover

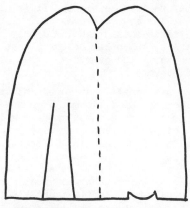

ONE-PIECE MOCCASIN PATTERN

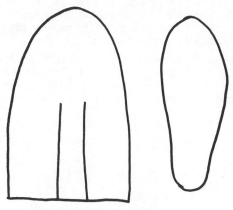

HARD-SOLED MOCCASIN PATTERN

all the exposed part of a leg beneath leggings or dress. They were long enough to overlap in front, and held down with long thongs that were wrapped several times around the ankles. Two to six inch ankle flaps were common on most old two-piece style moccasins, also, though modern pairs seldom have them. The flaps were generally made of undecorated hide, in Winter of fur, and in later years often of canvas. It is said that everyday moccasins around the turn of the century were often made of canvas throughout (with rawhide soles) but we have only seen a couple of pairs (one of which was fully beaded).

MOCCASIN DECORATIONS

Moccasins can be traditionally decorated in a variety of ways, including fringing, beading, painting, and adding fur or cloth. A common detail on Blackfoot moccasins is the fringed trailer that sticks out from the heel. Dr. Wissler looked at thirteen pairs of moccasins in 1910 and found that four had no trailer, three had one trailer, three had two trailers, and three had fringes all the way up the heel seam. This was done by adding a strip of hide, known as a welt, between the seam. Such a welt is often found between the side seam on one-piece moccasins, though rarely on hard-soled styles. A welt of wool is usually put into the seam between the moccasin and ankle flap. Often this welt is half an inch or an inch wide and sewn down with a cross stitch, or with appliqued beads, that makes it look very nice.

In 1833 Maximilian wrote that Blackfoot moccasins were often painted so that one foot was a different color than the other. This may have had some sacred purpose, though Ewers could find no one, in the 1940's, who knew anything about it. Medicine Pipe Owners and other Holy People have a tradition of painting both moccasins with sacred red Earth.

It is said that Blackfoot moccasins fully covered with quillwork or beadwork were not common, although many examples exist in museum collections. Most moccasins seem to have been decorated with small designs in the area between the toes and the instep. Characteristic designs include the "keyholes," crosswise bands, and variations of a three-pronged affair that is thought by many to represent the three basic divisions of the Blackfoot Nation. Bead and quill decorations are always applied to the moccasin tops before they are sewn to the bottoms. Turning a fully-beaded moccasin right side out, when it is completed, is a good test of the beadwork's durability.

In the past there was no particular difference between men's and women's moccasins, except that those worn by women always had ankle flaps, while those worn by men sometimes did not. Women's leggings fit snugly over these ankle flaps. In more recent years most women have adopted the high-top style of moccasin traditionally worn by other tribes. These come up to below the knee, and eliminate the need for separate leggings. Generally such high-top moccasins have flowers beaded on them--one on the toe and another fairly high up on the top flap. Children's moccasins are the same as those worn by adults, except smaller.

Drawings on this page represent a few of the most basic designs used on Blackfoot moccasins, according to a study made in the 1940's by John Ewers. Old People told him that the design in figure A is the most ancient of all. They called it the "crooked nose" design, and said that it was especially popular on the one-piece moccasins of Buffalo fur. It was commonly made with red and white quills, or with red and blue or red and yellow beads (mainly the old, large, "real beads").

The "keyhole" design in figure B was called "round" design. Sometimes the basic shape was cut out of trade cloth, sewn down, and only edged with beads. Often it was combined with a narrow band all the way around the bottom of the moccasin tops.

Figure C shows what was called the "cross" or "striped" design, which was generally made with the narrow band around the bottom of the moccasin, as shown. Ewers was told that red, yellow, and green were the favorite colors for this design.

While the first three figures show designs that were fairly common among tribes other than the Blackfoot, figure D shows one that seems to have been almost an exclusive Blackfoot design. Many variations existed, several of which show in the following photographs. Ewers said that this design was called "three finger Beadwork," "half breed work," or "white man sewing," and that the People he spoke to denied any tribal symbolism for the three fingers. Elderly Bloods have told us that the three points represent the three divisions, with a common origin from the Earth. They didn't say if this was an ancient tradition or a more recent conclusion, but the design, itself, is definately an ancient one. The area inside the rounded portion is commonly filled with red trade cloth.

Figure E shows a basic floral design, of which there are a great many variations. Some of the floral designs became very intricate after the coming of the small seed beads, in the 1870's.

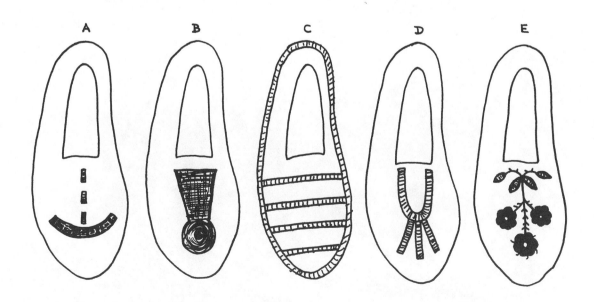

A   B   C   D   E

(All moccasins on this page at Heye)

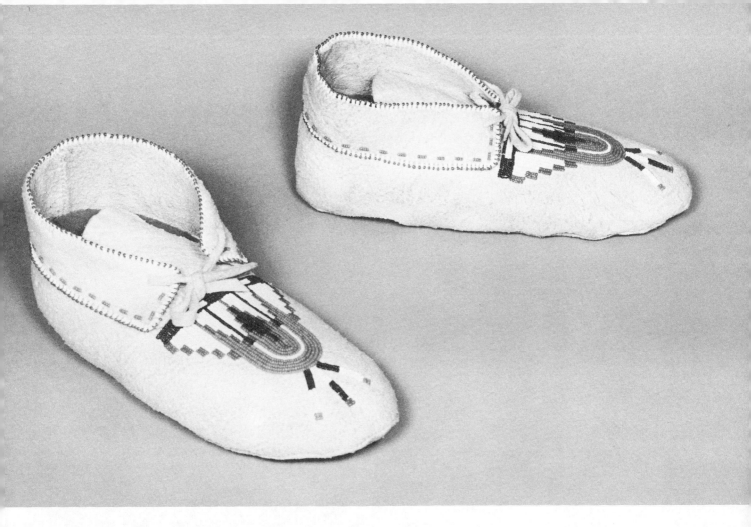

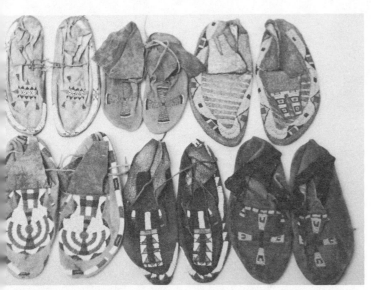

ABOVE: A recent pair of hard-soled moccasins, made of
white Deerskin and decorated with a modern version of a
traditional design. (MPI)
CENTER: Partly-beaded moccasins from around 1900. (Heye)
BOTTOM: Samples of a museum collection from the 1900's.
(Both at PMAA)

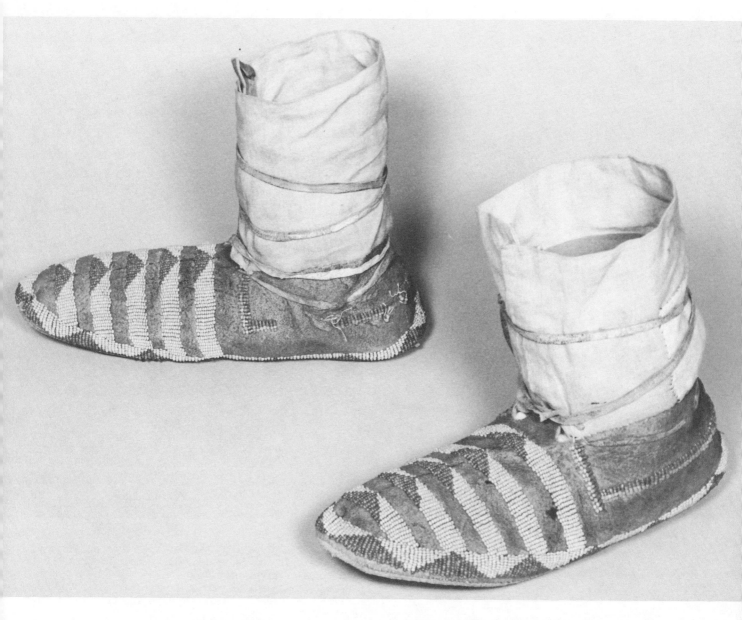

ABOVE: "Cross beadwork" design on hard-soled moccasins with canvas tops. (MPI)
BELOW: More examples of "cross beadwork" and a pair with "round beadwork." (Both at Heye)

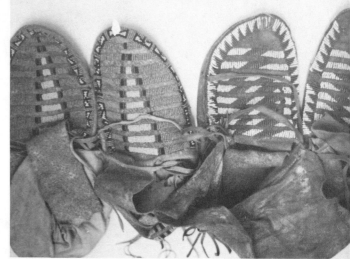

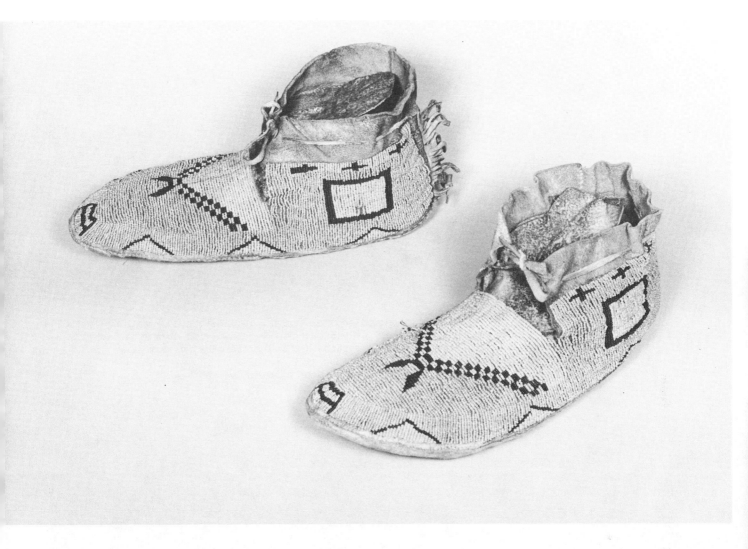

ABOVE: A pair of fully-beaded moccasins with fringes up the heel seam. Popular background colors for beading on moccasins include white, blue, green, and pink. (MPI)
BELOW LEFT: Fully-beaded moccasins with high tops and fringes along the seams. This pair was bought around
1920 and looks very new. (Heye)
BELOW RIGHT: Various designs on moccasins made in the later 1900's and bought in the 1960's. (PMAA)

11

ABOVE: The ultimate in beaded moccasins: fully beaded tops and soles! Collectors call this style "burial moccasin," on the assumption that such beadwork could only be worn by someone lying down in a casket. Actually, they were worn by proud and wealthy Persons to ceremonials and gatherings where most of the time was spent sitting down, with legs crossed and moccasin soles showing.
BELOW: Another design for fully beaded moccasins, with high tops of canvas. (Both MPI)

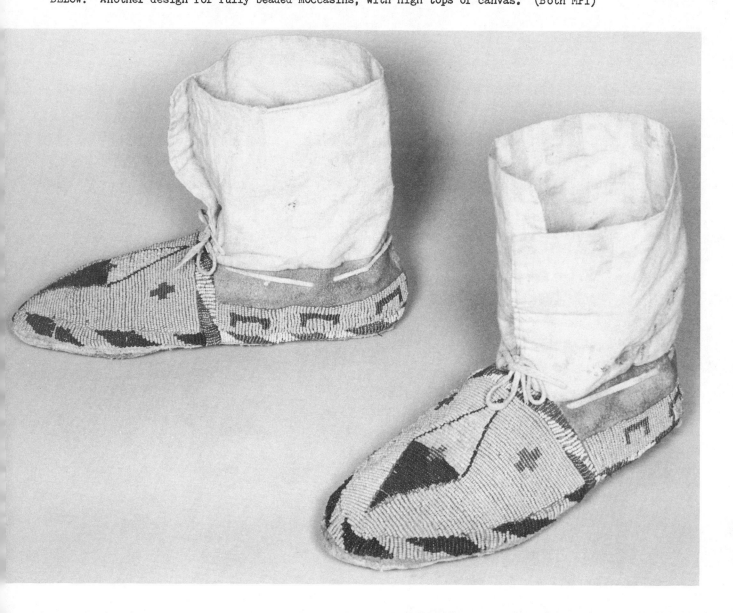

ABOVE: Another pair of ceremonial moccasins, literally fully beaded, including the long tongue.
BELOW: Fully beaded tops with a large floral design, of recent make. (Both MPI)

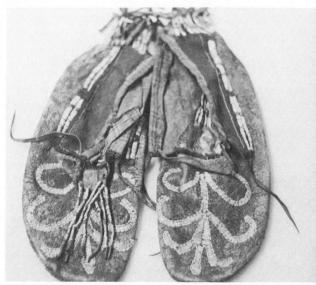

ABOVE: Recent moccasins, fully quilled over the front, worn by a man. (MPI)
CENTER: Old moccasins with two kinds of quillwork: sewn on top, and bound on sides and tongue strings. (Heye)
BOTTOM: An old pair with fully quilled tops and beaded strip around the bottom. The other, a very old pair, with bound quillwork sewn down in the center, and Real Beads sewn around for an edge. (Both at Heye)

14

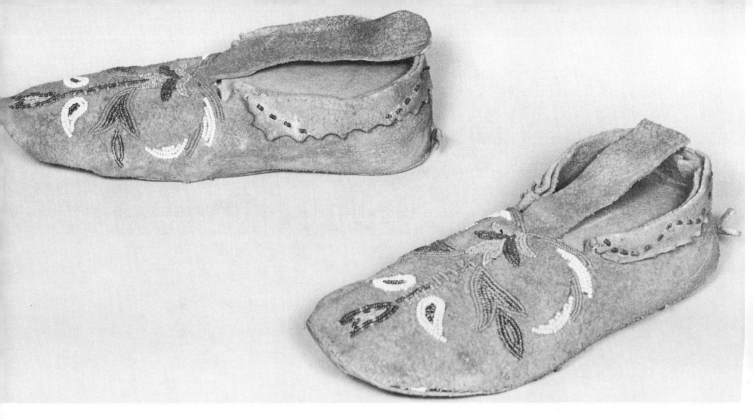

ABOVE: Partly-beaded moccasins with the old floral design, and a coating of sacred red paint for ceremonial wear. (MPI)

BELOW: Various floral designs on partly-beaded moccasins bought in the 1960's. (Both PMAA)

Various designs on women's high-top moccasins of recent make. (MPI above, PMAA below)

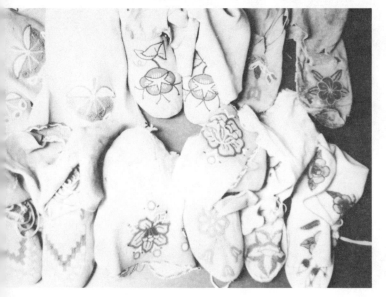

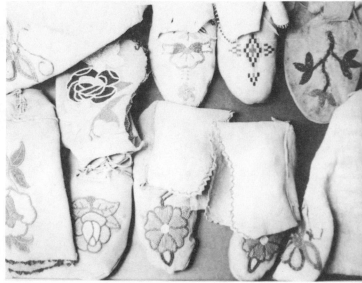

Men's Shirts

The following description of shirts and leggings gives us some idea of men's dress clothing worn in the early 1800's. According to Maximilian:

"The dress of the Blackfeet is made of tanned leather, and the handsomest leather shirts are made of the skin of the bighorn, which, when new, is of a yellowish-white colour, and looks very well. A narrow strip of the skin with the hair is generally left at the edge of such a skin. These shirts have half sleeves, and the seams are trimmed with tufts of human hair, or of horsehair dyed of various colours, hanging down, and with porcupine quills sewn round their roots. These shirts generally have at the neck a flap hanging down both before and behind, which we saw usually lined with red cloth, ornamented with fringe, or with stripes of yellow and coloured porcupine quills, or of sky-blue glass beads. Some have all these fringes composed of slips of white ermine; this is a very costly ornament, these little animals having become scarce. Many of the distinguished chiefs and warriors wore such dresses, which are really handsome, ornamented with many strings hanging down, in the fashion of a Hungarian tobacco pouch. When these leather shirts begin to be dirty, they are often painted of a reddish-brown colour; but they are much handsomer when they are new. Some of these Indians wear on the breast and back round rosettes like the Assiniboins, but this is only a foreign fashion, and the genuine Blackfoot costume has no such ornament. Their leggings are made like those of the other Missouri Indians, and ornamented, in the same manner, with tufts of hair or stripes of porcupine quills; the shoes, of buffalo or elk leather, are also adorned with porcupine quills, each having a ground of a different colour for its ornaments; thus if one is white, the other is yellow...."

The old style buckskin shirts were basically made from two large hides of Deer or Sheep. The hides were divided as in figure B. The larger section forms the body, while the shorter section is folded in half (along the dotted line) to make a sleeve. All the leg pieces were left on and fringed, and the tails were left, also. Figure C shows the main pieces, ready to put together. The sleeves were too short to cover the whole arm, leaving the hands free for work like hunting or fighting. The forelegs hung down by the wearer's armpits. The sleeves were sewn to the main body, which was also sewn across the shoulders. However, the sides were not sewn, but only tied together with thongs.

These old shirts always had quilled or beaded strips sewn down over the shoulders, and usually along the sleeves as well. All exposed edges were either fringed or notched. Common shirts had fringes along the bottoms of the sleeves. The average length of these was perhaps six or eight inches. Some tribes liked fringes a foot or two in length, but this was not a traditional Blackfoot style.

In addition to the common fringed shirts there used to be a great many Holy Shirts, decorated with Weasel skins or hairlocks. Such shirts can usually be recognized by their coatings of Sacred Paint--red or yellow--which was applied during and after special ceremonies of initiation. This is the significance of Earth-coated shirts, mentioned above by Maximilian, not the fact that they began to "get dirty." Those without paint are simply common shirts, not ceremonial ones.

Figure A shows the basic pattern of a more recent buckskin shirt. By 1900 even the hind legs were generally cut off, so that shirts began to look very tailored.

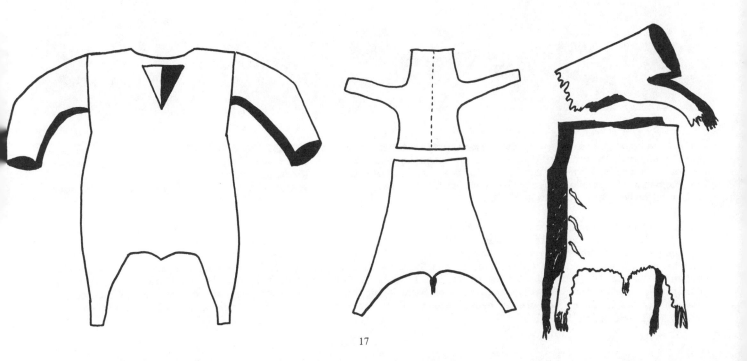

This is a good photo to study for details of stitches of various kinds. Notice that the beaded strips are on canvas, and that the edging around the neck is reinforced with buckskin lacing. In later years the hairlocks were donated by friends and relatives and did not represent scalps taken by the owner. Hairlock Shirts were always sacred articles requiring transfer, but any buckskin shirt could be decorated with some locks of hair, just for style. (MPI)

Neck openings on traditional shirts are just slits left open at the top. Thongs on each side are used to tie this shut when the shirt is worn. This slit is usually edged with red cloth, which is then bound with a buckskin thong for extra wear. Some shirts have triangular flaps sewn to the bottoms of the slits. They are of cloth, half red and half black. Usually they have an edging of buckskin fringe, as well as beaded borders and stripes. Sometimes the cloth is all red, in the shape of a rectangle, with beaded borders and stripes. More common than the cloth patches were beaded or quilled rosettes, often five or six inches in diameter, one in front and one in back. Shirts look about the same from either side--only dried food stains might tell you which is which!

ABOVE: One of the most ancient Blackfoot shirts still in existance, this one dates back to around 1800.
It comes from a time when only great warriors and chiefs wore such shirts. The hairlocks came from fallen enemies, the parallel lines represented major coups, and the war scene was probably one for which the
shirt's owner was most noted. The well-worn quillwork strips are edged with the large, old-style beads
that were, then, rare and valuable. The hairlocks are also wrapped with quills. (Heye)
BELOW: Two more very old war shirts dating from the mid-1800's. Both of them are longer than most women's
dresses collected from that period. Notice that they both combine hairlocks with buckskin fringes, and
that the hides were left whole, including legs and tails. (Heye)

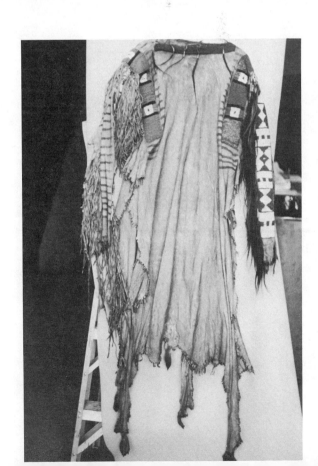

19

Painted Weasel Shirts

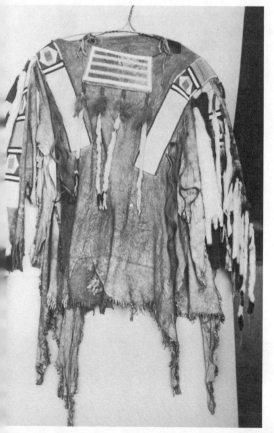

Weasel-tail Shirts are among the finest articles of dress worn by traditional men of the Blackfoot Nation. Most men of importance owned one or more of these shirts during their lifetime, although there are less than a dozen left among the People, today. Most of these shirts that were not worn to the graves by their last owners were quickly sold for high prices by their inheritors.

Although anyone may decorate a buckskin shirt with Weasel skins, most of these shirts were considered to be sacred articles that were ceremonially transferred. Only transferred shirts could be covered with sacred paint (usually yellow or red) and with other painted symbols, such as the parallel lines, circles, claw marks, and tadpole (or Water Bug) designs. Songs and facial paintings accompany the transfer. The transferred shirts (and leggings) are kept in rawhide cases and hung up with other Medicines. Daily incense is made for them. Only two such transfers have taken place in recent years.

Both shirts on this page were made sacred by transfer. The one above is a more recent version (MPI), while the one on the left was purchased in 1923 and may well have been used in war (Heye).

20

This style of garment is known as a Holy Shirt, both literally and spiritually. There were basically three reasons for the existance of such shirts: As transferred articles, used mainly for Power in battle; for part of the regalia worn by certain members (known as Bear Braves) of certain societies; and as expressions of certain visions and dreams which directed the making and designing of such garments. The latter reason caused the existance of a number of these shirts during the early Reservation Period. Most of these later versions were made of cloth, and the holes often represented the Power of Hail. The earlier shirts were usually made of buckskin, and the marks represented bullet holes. In one variation the holes formed a pattern representing a Christian cross, while on another such crosses were put on with sacred paint. That style became known as the Lord's Shirt. Other variations had feathers, hairlocks, and symbols of Powers attached. The one here pictured is of cloth. (MPI)

Above is an example of a fancy buckskin shirt that could be made and worn by anybody, even though it has some hairlock and Weasel skin decorations like the sacred shirts requiring a ceremonial transfer. Notice the neat tailoring and sewing, with no rough parts of the hides left on. Such shirts were most always made of white buckskin. They were regularly cleaned with rough, white stones and sometimes had white Earth paint rubbed over them, as well. Chalk has been used for the same purpose, in more recent years, along with sandpaper and baking flour. The lady who beaded the strips for this shirt encountered a fairly common problem--she ran out of beads for her background before she finished the chore. When she went back to her bead source for more of the same color, she was given hanks from a different "run" than her first batch. The two probably looked alike in the store, but completed beadwork always brings out these slight variations that occur from one run to the next. When doing large areas of beadwork, try to have more beads on hand than you will need. (MPI)

At the left are three wing fans of the kind often carried by men in their ceremonial dress, especially on sacred occasions. At top is a Hawk wing, the other two are of Eagle. Other Bird wings were used, also. Some were used plain, some had simple wrappings for handles, and many were decorated with fancy handles of bead-covered buckskin or wool cloth, with hanging fringes or strips of Animal fur. (PMAA)

BELOW: Louis Champagne and wife, with Jim White Calf and wife, all dressed in their finest around 1935.

ABOVE: A buckskin shirt of the modern style, noticeable for its tailored appearance. This style has changed little since the turn of the century, except that commercially-tanned hides are often used now, instead of those tanned by hand. The beading is done in the applique style except for the border on the neck flap, which is done in lazy stitch. Today, such shirts are usually worn with matching leggings, gloves, and moccasins. This is called a "chief suit." (MPI)

LEFT: A well-worn buckskin jacket of an unusual style. It was obtained in Browning around 1920, and probably made many years before then. The beads on it are the larger kind used most commonly before the 1870's, and on women's dresses after that. They were used here either because the jacket is very old, or because its maker did not want to spend much time beading it. Notice that it only buttons part way down the front, then has an added section sewn on like a tail-coat. This section is edged with trade-cloth (nearly worn-off), and has pockets with beaded and fringed flaps. (Heye)

On this page are two buckskin shirts decorated with Porcupine quillwork. The one above is an older style than the one below, which was probably made after 1900. It is hard to tell where shirts of this kind were made, since many tribes used them for wear and for impressive gifts to visitors. (MPI)

On these two pages are men's jackets that combine leather with fur. Such combinations are rare in collections of Blackfoot work, though they are common among the People who live in the cold Far North. On this page are the jacket fronts, while on the opposite page are the backs.

ABOVE: The two large photos show a shirt that came from Browning and was probably made around 1890 or 1900. At first glance it seems to be a typical Weasel Shirt, with the addition of an Otter hide. It is made of buckskin and tailored in the style between old and new. However, it is unusual for being made to button all the way down the front. The Otter skin is split in half, accordingly. It is sewn on so that the head hangs down in back and the tail hangs in front. Brass shoe buttons are sewn down the front as further decoration. The Weasel strips have bits of yarn and hackles added near the buckskin thongs, on which are strung pony beads.

It could be that the design of this shirt came to its owner in a dream, and that it was ceremonially transferred. However, it could just as well be that someone made up the shirt and wore it just for style. (MPI)

BOTTOM: This jacket is similar to those still made and worn in Canada, today. It is based on European styles and called "half-breed jacket" by the Old People. The fur on this one looks like Beaver, and the hide looks heavy enough to be Moose or Elk. It was bought on the Sarcee Reserve in the 1920's. and probably not made long before then. (Heye)

Above is a very ornate dress shirt made from woolen trade cloth. Its maker was obviously an artistic Person who combined several styles. The beadwork on the cuffs and collar is of a style seldom seen on Blackfoot craftwork, but very common among tribes far to the East. It is based on different colors of cloth. The combination of materials, here, is similar to that on trade cloth dresses. (MPI)

ABOVE: Two trade cloth shirts made for boys. Notice how both styles are variations of old-time buck-skin shirts. One is decorated with buckskin fringe, ribbons, and brass buttons. The other has ribbons and strips of Weasel skin. We know of one case where such a shirt was transferred to a young boy along with a Medicine Pipe Bundle. Our uncle once received such a shirt as a gift from the Sioux. (Heye)

BELOW: Another dress shirt of trade cloth. Usually these shirts were red, blue, or green. (MPI)

A boy's Hairlock Shirt from the early 1900's. Children of wealthy families were often given small versions of fancy dresses and buckskin suits, sometimes complete with the transfer ceremonial. The stripes painted on this shirt signify that it was a sacred article. The imperfect workmanship is much more noticeable in this photo than it was when the shirt was being worn. (MPI)

ABOVE LEFT: A boy's dress shirt that was ceremonially transferred and painted, even though it has neither Weasel nor hairlock decorations. The painting was probably a blessing bestowed on the boy by some noted old warrior or Holy Man. This is an older style shirt, from the 1800's. The triangular neck flap is of wool, half red and half black. The colors have spiritual significance. Notice the unusual sleeve strips, which are of white beads with a narrow border but no other design. (Heye)

ABOVE RIGHT: A long coat of smoked buckskin, obtained in Browning during the early 1900's. It may have been obtained as a gift, since it is of a style worn by tribes far to the East. However, its maker may have been influenced by some coat seen on a Person from the East. The beaded designs are unusual, also. (Heye)

RIGHT: Part of a display on the Blackfoot Tribe in the Museum of the American Indian, in New York City. At the bottom is a fine Weasel-tail Shirt. Above it is a nicely-beaded bag of some kind. The knife sheath on the upper right was made for dress wear. The pattern of beadwork was popular for a time in the early 1900's. (Heye)

BLANKET COAT

Blanket coats were called Capotes by the early French trappers who introduced them to the Blackfoot country. Most Capotes seem to have been made from striped Hudson's Bay blankets, though we've seen all sorts of other patterns in old photos, as well. Every Blackfoot man seemed to have one of these, during the past 100 years or more. Even today they are common, especially at dances, where they form a simple outfit, in combination with moccasins and a sash.

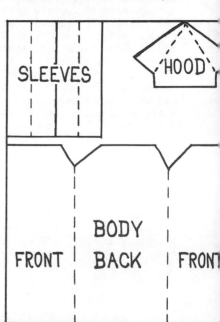

SLEEVES

HOOD

BODY

FRONT   BACK   FRONT

32

Vests

The custom of wearing vests is said to have been adopted from the early settlers. Store-bought cloth vests were commonly worn plain, or with some beading of floral designs. These were most popular around the turn of the century. Leather vests were patterned after cloth ones, but seldom worn plain. The finest vests had fully-beaded fronts (usually of convas, with floral designs), with plain or partly-beaded backs (of buckskin), and colorful linings of calico cloth. Blackfoot vests rarely had shell or ribbon decorations, like those of some other tribes.

On this page are the four common styles of decorated vests. Clockwise, from above, they are: Fully beaded front, cloth back, and calico lining, from the Bloods (Heye); fully-beaded front with geometric design (PMAA); partly-beaded buckskin with spots of green paint (AMNH); and store-bought cloth with partly-beaded flowers.

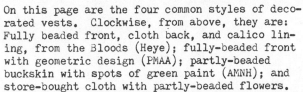

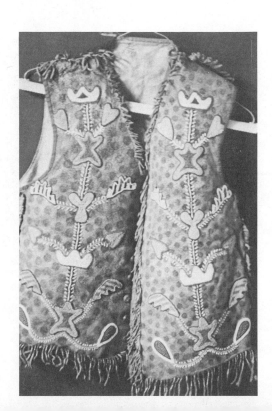

Above is a fully-beaded vest, with cloth back, made around 1915, in Browning. The fringe is
from some drapes, or a bedspread. In floral work, like this, the designs are beaded first
and the background is filled in later. The letters "B.H." stand for Buffalo Hide, the name
of a Piegan family. (MPI) The same vest is seen on the opposite page, in the left portrait.
It is being worn by Fish Wolf Robe, around 1920. Several old photos show him wearing this
vest, so it may have belonged to him at one time. He is also wearing a popular-style choker
of brass beads and cowrie shells along with a fully-beaded "tie and collar" that was popular
in the early 1900's in imitation of commercial business suits. This man always wore Otter
fur braid wraps in a style that was most popular among tribes further East. The man next
to him is Irwin Little Plume, who was noted for his fancy dressing. (Photos from Glacier
Studio) The vest on the opposite page is of cloth, with very ornate flowers. (MPI)

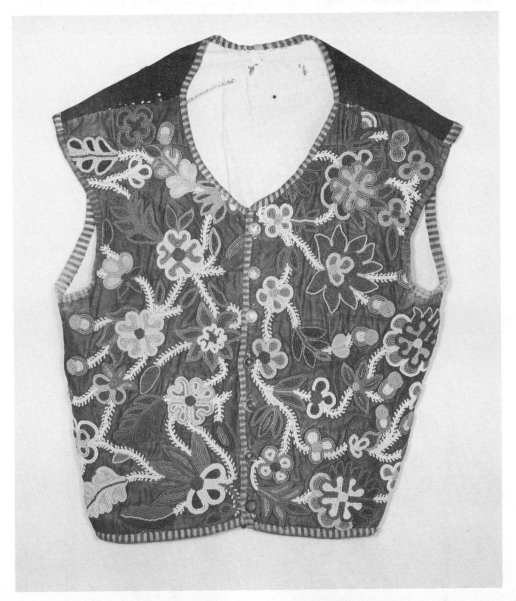

The flowers on this fine vest are beaded very intricately in many different colors. The background color is white, which was most common. Light blue was the other favorite. (MPI)

A man's vest of buckskin, partly beaded with flowers, and lined with cloth for extra strength. Vests like this were made for boys, too. They were worn primarly at dances. (MPI)

Below is an Eagle-tail fan of the kind often carried at dances by men and women. Such fans were made from complete tails and from individual tailfeathers tied together to look like tails. Handles were made of rawhide or pieces of wood, covered with buckskin or wool cloth and often beaded fully or partially. (Heye)

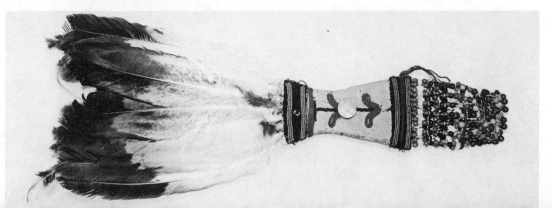

Leggings

Men's traditional leggings are basically tubes of buckskin long enough to reach from the ankles to the hips. At the outside, top, each legging has a strap by which it is tied to the man's belt. The leggings usually matched the shirt, in design and decorations, when a new suit was made. However, leggings wore out much sooner than shirts, so that unmatched suits were common. Many sacred shirts were transferred without leggings, for this reason. Ordinary leggings were then used, instead. The making of each hide legging requires nearly a whole hide. As with shirts, old-time leggings utilized the natural shape of a hide, with the legs fringed and left on for decoration. Old-time leggings often drug on the ground, but later styles were tailored for straight, ankle-length cuffs and even side seams. At the bottom right is a pair of leggings of the very old style, made around 1800. (Heye) Next to them is a pair of ordinary buckskin leggings from the early 1900's. Above that are two more buckskin leggings, with the very popular beaded rectangular panels. Finally, there is a pair of blue blanket leggings of recent style. (Heye)

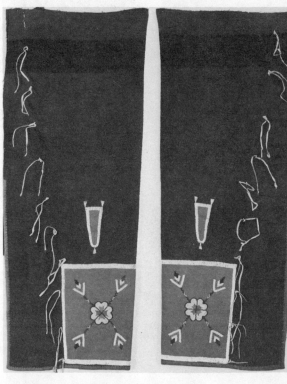

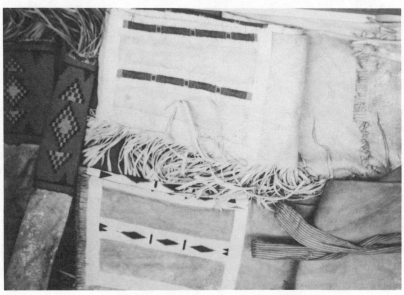

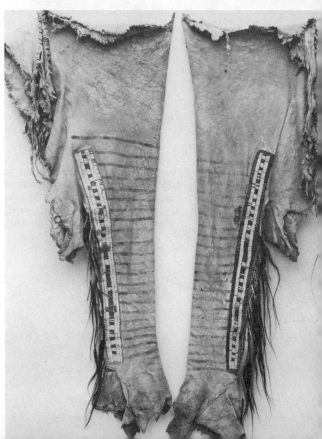

Below is a pair of buckskin leggings from the later 1800's. The natural shape of the hides can still be recognized, but the legging style is much more tailored than the very old pair on the opposite page. Beaded strips take the place of the quilled ones, although a few Real Beads can be seen on the quilled strips, where they were added during repairs. Both pairs of leggings are decorated with hairlocks and were worn with matching shirts by noted warriors. The black stripes represent major coups of the original owners.

The beaded strips on this pair of leggings have one of the most common design combinations--the "mountain" design along with the crosses. Other popular styles include the bar and cross, the elongated feathers, and the rectangular boxes. All of these, of course, are made up of smaller designs, within. Old-style shirt and legging strips were usually about two inches wide, with narrow borders. Later, the strips got wider and the borders were often left off. White and light blue were the most common background colors. (MPI)

The pair of leggings on this page were probably part of a complete Weasel suit, made sacred by ceremonial transfer, although there are no stripes or other symbols, and it's hard to tell if the hide has been painted. They were made in the early 1900's, and have the wide beaded strips with no borders. The narrow, beaded bands are unusual, though evidently inspired by the beaded panels used on ordinary leggings. Note how much more tailored this pair of leggings is compared to the two old ones with hairlock fringes. The cuffs are edged with red wool and buckskin thongs. Red yarn is attached to the Weasel skins. (MPI)

The leggings of an ordinary buckskin suit, with a few Weasel skins added for decoration. These leggings were held up by the long straps hanging down from the upper corners. (MPI)

Dresses

The basic style of traditional dresses worn by Blackfoot women must have become popular sometime around 1800. David Thompson, a trader and explorer, wrote in the 1780's that dresses were then much like modern women's slips--a rectangular body held up with shoulder straps, to which separate sleeves were added in cooler weather. Women of neighboring tribes wore similar dresses, though no Blackfoot examples exist in museum collections, today.

The style of dress which is still worn by some women on special occasions, today, has a cape sewn to the main piece so that the complete dress covers the whole body, including the shoulders and upper arms. At least two large Deerhides are required for its making.

Dresses were made with the heads of the hides at the bottoms. The necks and forelegs were left in their natural shapes, to give the dresses the characteristic wavy bottoms. These were usually fringed.

Tops of dresses had several variations. In the most common method they were cut nearly straight across, then joined together by a third piece, the yoke. This was in the shape of a long rectangle, as in figure A of the drawings. Figure B shows the general shape of the dress-top, with the yoke attached, while figure C shows the method most commonly used to connect the yoke with the front and back. Often the yoke was made by joining together the two strips cut off the rear end of the hides in tailoring the main part of the body. Sometimes two large hides were sewn together so that the last few inches could be folded down, front and back, and stitched in place like the separate yoke. Some dresses have no yoke at all, but are simply made by sewing two hides together with the top part tailored for the shoulders and arms. Modern buckskin dresses, like shirts and leggings, are notable for being very tailored. They usually lack the legs and other natural shapes, while their fringes are generally very neat and even.

Several kinds of stitches were popular for sewing up buckskin dresses. Seams used for the tops were generally turned inside when completed. On the sides, however, they were often left exposed, some distance in from the edge of the hide, with the remaining flap cut into short fringes. Often welts were inserted in the side seams and then fringed. A triangular piece of hide was often sewn in between the seam, toward the bottom of a dress, to make the skirt fuller. Notice that the bottoms of sleeves are not sewn shut.

As with moccasins and other articles of hide that were to be decorated, skins used for dresses were worn with the flesh side out. Close examination shows that most dresses have pieces of skin added in various places to fill out the hides. On those dresses where the rear end of the hide hangs down in front, forming the yoke, the Deer tail is generally still attached--at least a clipped version of it. It hangs down in the center of the chest and behind. At other times Deer tails were simply sewn on in the same place. This is all the decoration seen on some dresses, along with the abundant fringing.

Most dresses in museum collections are also decorated with beadwork, pieces of trade cloth, and items like shells, teeth, and thimbles. It is through these decorations that we can best tell Blackfoot dresses from those of other tribes. Noted characteristics include a curve in the breastband beading that resembles the shape of a Deerhide's rear end (as it looks when folded over for a yoke), a triangular symbol at the lower front (with an ancient significance of womanhood), and two other symbols, lower down (said by some to represent the kidneys, though their original meanings may be lost in time).

Beadwork on old dresses was done with Real Beads, or pony beads, usually in lazy stitch. The breastband is usually in two colors, like black and white, light blue and white, or pink and green. Dark and light colors were usually combined for contrast. Sometimes the colored

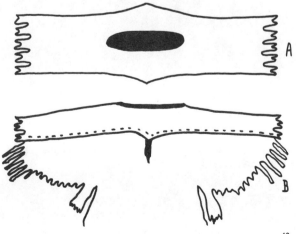

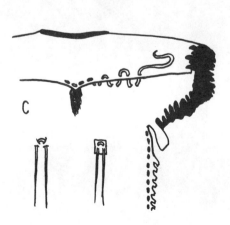

stripes were broken up with small geometric sections, but rarely with any other designs. However, designs--and additional colors--were often
used on the shoulder bands that became popular on
these kinds of dresses after the small seed beads
became available. Narrow, beaded strips along
the bottoms of these dresses were also popular.
The patches at the bottoms of most dresses were
generally made of trade cloth, one side red and
the other black or dark blue. These were often
edged with beads, also. In addition, little pieces of trade cloth were used to back the many buckskin strands hanging down from different parts of
dresses. Long ago dresses were decorated with
quillwork in place of beads.

The first cloth dresses were generally made of
red or blue wool. This tended to stretch or
ravel, unless it was used in more square shapes.
The selvedge edge (the white strip, where the
cloth was clamped during dying) was utilized to
decorate the bottoms of most cloth dresses. In
addition, beadwork was usually applied with Real
Beads or seed beads. In some cases the beadwork
was in the form of the old breastband, in others
it was only a small strip along the shoulders,
and in still others it covered the whole top.
A new style of decoration became popular, in
which rows of beadwork alternated with rows of
cowrie shells or, sometimes, Elk teeth. This
style was especially common on lighter cloth
dresses that were quite in style from the 1890's
until the 1920's. The beadwork on these dresses
was often done with large, tubular shaped beads
known as "basket beads." The bottoms of these
dresses were quite full, and usually decorated
with many parallel rows of ribbons in different
widths and colors. Sateen was a popular material
for these lighter dresses, and many different colors were used. They were usually sewn with a
sewing machine, and neatly hemmed. The sleeves
were sewn shut all the way, and the tops were
often lined on the inside to support the beads
and shells.

The widespread use of cloth brought on many new
variations to women's dresses. One popular style
used a cape, decorated with beadwork or shells,
that could be worn over any plain calico dress.
Some capes were actually the decorated remnants
of worn-out cloth dresses. Some cloth dresses
were decorated with buckskin additions that were
fringed. Some dresses were made of velvet, with
decorations of ribbons and metal sequins. The
most valuable dresses had their tops covered with
Elk teeth or cowrie shells.

The two photos on the right were taken in the
1920's. The upper one shows the wife of Bird
Rattler, wearing a tailored buckskin dress that
combines old styles with new. It has the curved
breastband in two colors, made with the more re-
cently-used seed beads. It has a neck and shoulder band, as well as fringes strung with basket
beads and thimbles. The sleeves are sewn shut
on the bottom and not fringed on the ends.

The lower photo shows the wife of Irwin Little
Plume, wearing a cloth dress of the style that
was real popular from about 1890 to 1920. It is
decorated with rows of basket beads, pony beads,
and cowrie shells. (Glacier Studio Photos)

ABOVE: Two plain buckskin dresses of the old style, with added yokes. The one on the right was painted.
BELOW: At left is a dress from the Bloods, beaded with the large Real Beads. Necklace beads and thimbles hang from the thongs below the breastband. At right is a girl's dress from the Siksikai, bought in Gleichen in 1923. Note the front triangle, here made in the shape of a heart. (All from Heye)

ABOVE: At left, a dress decorated with seed beads and Elk teeth. At right, one with painted stripes.
BELOW: Two old style dresses with more than average beadwork on the shoulders. (All from Heye)

ABOVE: Two wool dresses from around 1900. The one on the left is
blue, edged with cloth and ribbon, and decorated with cowrie shells.
The one on the right is red, with beaded yoke and buckskin fringe.
BELOW: A red wool dress from the Bloods, probably made about 1910.
The applique beadwork is backed on the inside. (All at Heye)

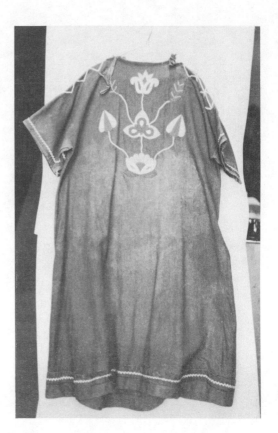

ABOVE: Two views of a buckskin dress made around 1900, and bought in Browning in 1923. The breastband is of different-colored "basket beads", while the neck and shoulders have real beads. Note how the dress looks more "squared" and lacks some of the old decorations. BELOW: At left is another turn-of-the-century dress, fairly plain. In the center is an older style dress with only cloth patches and fringe for decorations. On the right is a girl's dress of a very simple style, made from two average-sized Deerhides. (All at Heye)

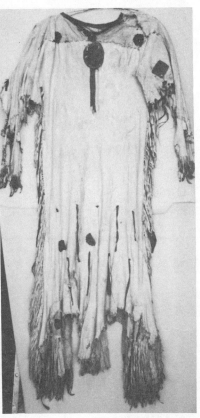

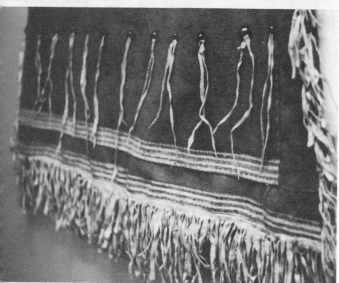

ABOVE: An old cloth cape, made around 1900, with basket bead decoration, has here been sewn to the top of a newly-made buckskin skirt. Sometimes such capes were worn over new cloth dresses, also. (MPI)

LEFT: Several photos showing two trade cloth dresses made around 1900. Both have rows of lazy-stitch beadwork, using seed beads. Also, both have buckskin fringes and pieced bottoms for style. The upper dress has two sections of selvedge edge along the bottom. The lower dress has one section of selvedge edge and then a strip of different-colored cloth. It also has elaborate and colorful beading that came into style with these wool dresses. Both dresses were sewn by hand. (Both at LM)

ABOVE: Close-up of a cloth dress decorated with basket beads, in the style of the turn-of-the-century. Some of the cloth seems to have been replaced on top of the original canvas backing. (MPI)

RIGHT: Some examples of belts worn by Blackfoot women with traditional style dresses. Early decorations consisted of brass buttons and brass tacks, with their points cut off. Most belts in museum collections are made of commercial heavy leather, such as that used on harnesses. The average width is four inches. Later belt decorations included fully beading, in applique stitch, and partly beading in long, loose rows of lazy stitch, usually combined with sections of tacks. (PMAA)

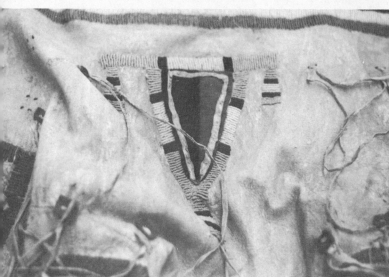

The photos on this page show the top and bottom of a buckskin dress that was probably made around 1900. It is of the old pattern, but with a more modern style of beadwork. The breastband is straight across, of seed beads in lazy stitch. The neck and shoulder bands are of the kind used on men's shirts, which is unusual. They are done in applique stitch. Also unusual are the strips of Weasel skin that hang down below the breastband. Women seldom used them, since they are a symbol of cunning and bravery among the warriors. Other hanging decorations on this dress include white-centered necklace beads and thin brass coils, made by wrapping brass wire tightly around a slim stick. Such coils were used on hairlocks and necklaces, also. (LM)

The sketch below shows another pattern for a buckskin dress, illustrating how such dresses were typically pieced together for lack of suitable large hides. Sides of buckskin dresses were sewn up to the armpits except when the wearer was a nursing mother, in which case the sewing stopped at the breastline.

Knife Cases

The knife cases on this page are the standard Blackfoot type, worn with a belt through the triangular opening. They were made of rawhide, either laced shut (as on top), or riveted (as on bottom). (Both MPI) The center photos show the fronts and backs of two cases obtained on the Blood Reserve before 1905. (PMAA) Beadwork, brass tacks, and red wool edging was the common decoration. Other shapes of knife cases included the fully-beaded dagger sheaths with "Beavertail" tabs on the bottom, as well as some made from buckskin and even Deer's feet with the hair left on.

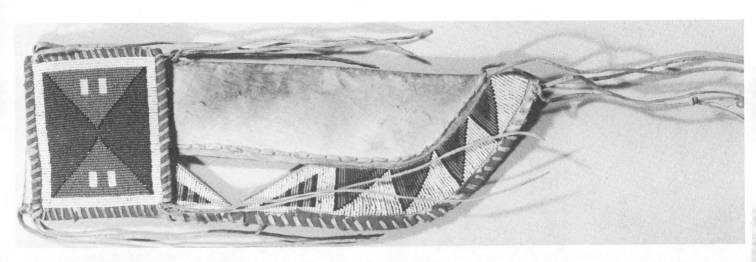

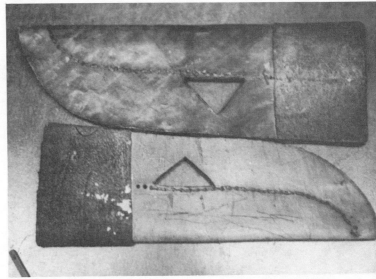

51

Women's Leggings

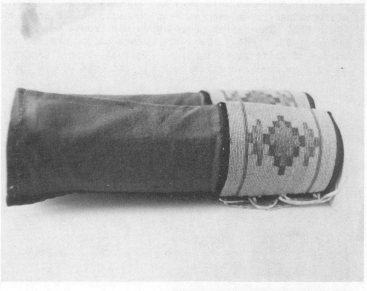

Leggings were always worn by Blackfoot women until the high-top moccasins of other tribes were adopted in the early 1900's. A plain style of legging is said to have been of undecorated skin or cloth, reaching from just below the knees to inside the flaps of the moccasins. Dress leggings, however, were well decorated with fully-beaded panels which were worn over the ankle flaps of moccasins, as in the photo above. (Heye) The beadwork is done on hide or canvas, while the tops are of wool, usually red, blue, or green. The openings of these leggings are worn to the outsides of the legs. They are usually closed with tie strings, but sometimes with brass shoe buttons. The edges overlap to the rear.

Below, a legging pattern.

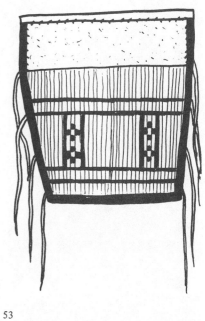

53

Robes

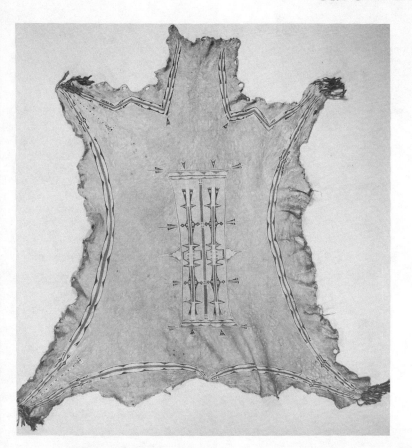

On this page are illustrated two styles of decorated robes. At the left is a fully-tanned Elk hide with painted designs of different colors. It came from the Bloods. (Heye) Below is a robe with beaded stripes of different colors. (MPI) On the next page is a beaded strip of the kind used on wool blankets. Similar strips of beadwork or quillwork were formerly used on robes, also, though they were usually wider and separated by two rosettes instead of four. At the bottom is a beaded blanket strip sewn to a "point blanket" (the three small stripes are "points" in trader's language). In this case the blanket was a Medicine Robe, decorated by its owner as directed in dreams. Several such Medicine Robes existed among the Blackfoot Nation as transferable articles. Some were used by Weather Dancers in the Sun Dance, while others were worn to ceremonies. (Both MPI)

Robes and blankets were always worn so that their decorated stripes run horizontal, from head to tail. Robes were worn with the heads to the left and the tails to the right. Blankets were worn so that the beaded strips went around the waist. There are many variations with blanket decorating and wearing, and even more with the use of the old-time robes.

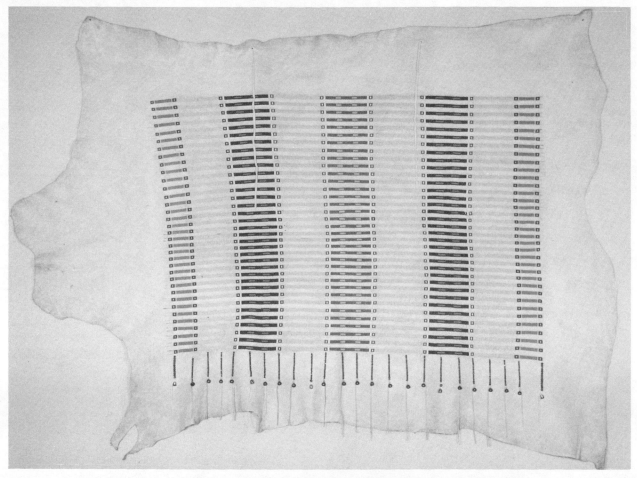

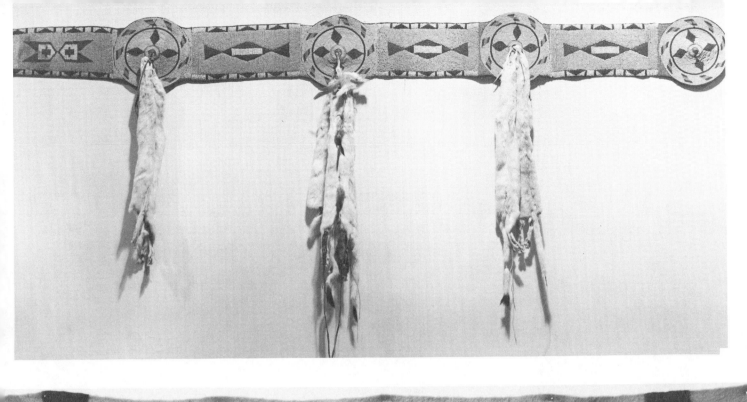

Necklaces

Necklaces were so popular and varied that these photos can only show a few of the many examples. Ancient necklaces were made from such materials as claws, bones, shells, seeds, and dried berries. In the early 1700's some necklaces started having imported beads on them, obtained in trade from other

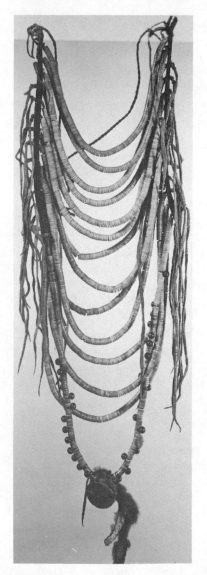

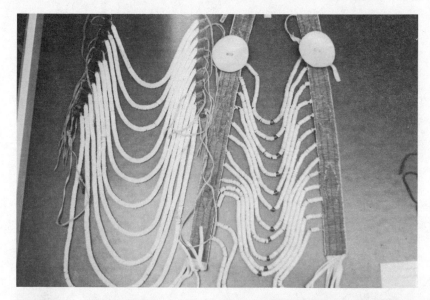

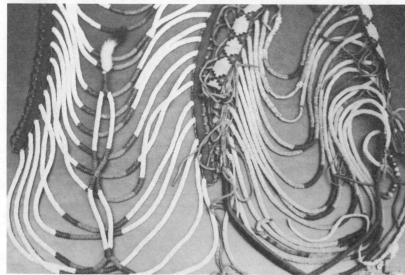

ABOVE: A fine loop-necklace of shell beads, or "wampum", with brass buttons mixed in. These are valuable beads. (Heye)

ABOVE RIGHT: Two kinds of loop-necklaces. Those on top are of strung disc beads (left) and shell beads (right). Those on the bottom are of wrapped seed beads. (Both at PMAA)

BOTTOM: A choker-necklace combination, with wrapped seed beads and a hairlock (left), and a Bear-claw choker (right) on a red, puckered wool strip with bead spacers. Gold rings are tied on at each end. The rosette is from a shirt. (LM)

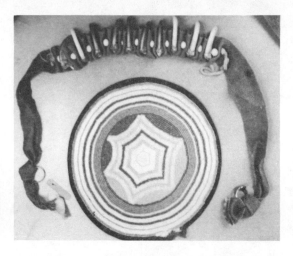

tribes. After that, glass and metal beads were used on practically every kind of necklace. However, the hair pipes that became so popular among many tribes for chokers and breastplates were hardly used among the Blackfoot People, at all. Instead of bone breastplates, the Blackfoot style was a long necklace of loops, usually bound with seed beads, held together by a narrow strap on each side. In place of bone chokers, the styles were strings of beads and cowrie shells, glass tube beads, and narrow strips of beadwork. Many necklaces were personal Medicines, and others were transferable Medicines. There are yet many elderly People among the Blackfoot Nation with rights to such transferable necklaces, including Buffalo Stones, Medicine Pipe shells, and Sundance hairlocks. Ask one of the Elders, if this interests you. The necklace can be remade, if it has been lost, as long as the owner still has the transferable rights. These can belong to men and women, and even children.

57

ABOVE: At left are two chokers of tubular glass beads, with smaller beads as spacers, and one beaded choker with a row of cowrie shells and an imitation "tie" drop. The style was also common without the "tie." At right are several necklaces of "toe bones" with beads. BELOW RIGHT: Two museum drawers of various necklaces, including shells, Bear and Eagle claws, Elk teeth, vertebra bones, antler tips, and stones. Some of these are sacred necklaces. (All at PMAA) CENTER: An old necklace of Buffalo teeth and early trade beads of glass. (Heye) LEFT: A woman's beaded necklace for her sewing kit. The tubular container was for her awl, the rectangular one for her thread and needles. Men used similar necklaces to carry their "toiletries"--mirror, paint, and comb. Others used them to hold their ration cards. (MPI)

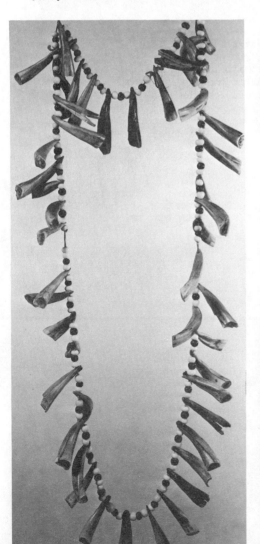

Hair Ornaments

Most Blackfoot hair ornaments were personal Medicines made up from directions given in dreams. Bunches of feathers, strips of fur, and round discs of metal and shell were the most common parts. They were tied in all different places on the head or braids. Single Eagle feathers worn in back of the head were popular among tribes other than the Blackfoot. The Old People had many different ways of wearing their long hair, which was an ornament, in itself. An article known as a "Matted Hair" was especially popular with school boys and those who had cut their hair short. It was made of human or Buffalo hair, matted and glued together, and fastened to a rawhide strip which was decorated. This was worn down the back. Many hair ornaments were fastened to store-bought hats, later on.

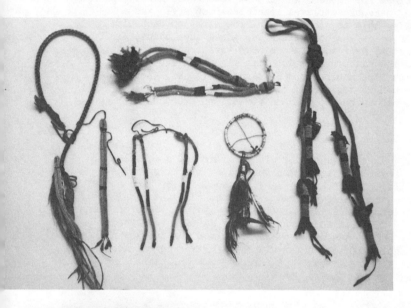
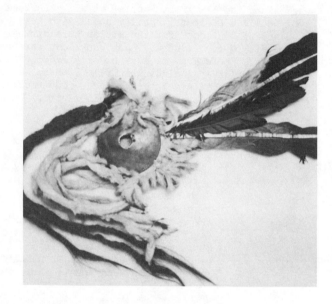

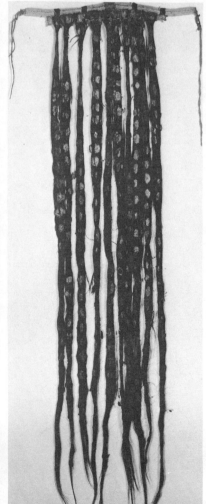

Clockwise, beginning at upper left: Some beaded braid attachments, along with a quilled, round headpiece; a personal Medicine worn at the back of the head; a similar one, from Sik-sikai; a "Matted Hair" ornament worn down the back; another one, with very long hair, held together with spots of pitch or glue. The thongs tie over the forehead. (All at Heye)

Headdresses

There are basically two kinds of traditional Blackfoot headdresses, one made with Weasel skins and the other with black and white Eagle feathers. Both styles are considered sacred. Although anyone may make them, they can be worn only by Persons ceremonially initiated. We present a picture of each kind here with the hope of inspiring a few of you to seek out one of the few remaining Persons who have the rights to perform such ceremonial initiations. These are People who have gone through such an initiation, themselves. Only a few of these headdresses remain among the Blackfoot Nation, and most of these are owned by members of the sacred Horns Society among the Bloods. The common Eagle feather headdresses of nowadays were adopted from the Sioux People in the 1890's.

LEFT: A very ornate Eagle feather head-dress of the old style, known as Straight-Up Headdress. The feathers are decorated with Horsehair, Weaselskin, and strips of quillwork. They were still common during the 1920's. (MPI)

BELOW: A horned Weasel Headdress, with a long trailer. (Heye)

Cradle Boards

Traditional Blackfoot mothers carried their babies in cradle boards like the ones on these two pages. The frame for one of these used to be made out of willows, curved and cross-braced, and later out of a large, sturdy board sawed to the desired shape. The buckskin covering was made in several pieces. The headboard section was often partly or fully beaded on the front. It was sewn at the edges to the large piece of hide that covered the whole back and sometimes wrapped around to the lower front. Patches and variations in the design were common. Some had an interior lining of fur. Some had hoods that could be laced snug to the baby's face. Some had decorated aprons over the bottom lacings. There was a sturdy strap fastened across the upper back, at left and right, in such a way that it could be worn by the mother on her back, with the strap across her shoulders. By this strap it was also hung from low tree limbs and from the pommel on a saddle. Lace-up bags without wooden frames were also used. (All MPI)

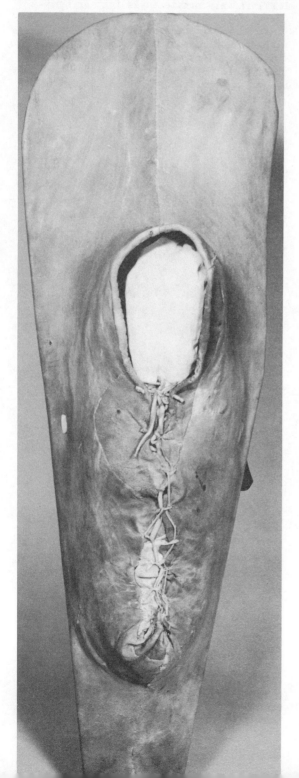
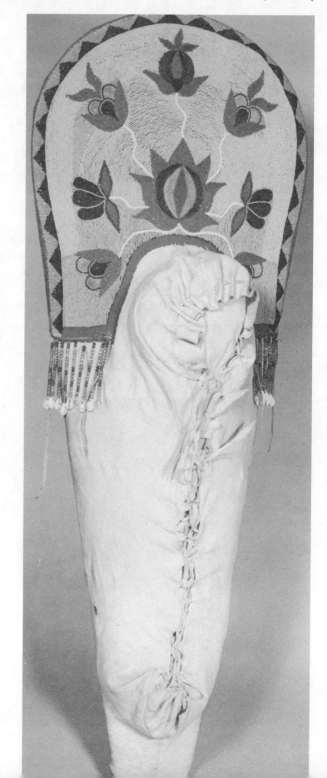

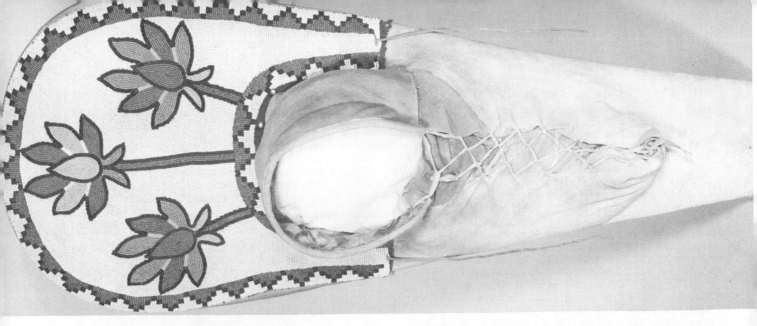

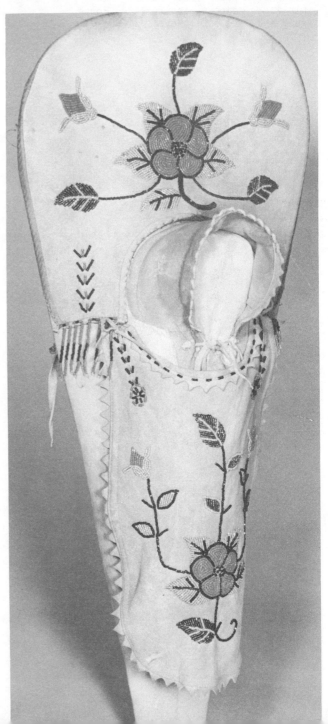

Toys

There were many traditional Blackfoot toys for children, although few remain in museum collections, today, and no one has ever written an account of their history or their making. Simple toys were made from sticks and bones and other natural articles, while some complex toys were exact replicas of articles used by adults, only in miniature. For instance, both boys and girls were given dolls of all kinds. Some were carved willow sticks, with cut-off branches for arms and legs. Others were made of soft buckskin, stuffed with hair gathered from many combings, and often dressed in fully-beaded clothing. Older girls were given dolls like the man and woman on these two pages, along with miniature articles for them to use--tipi, cooking gear, and even miniature Medicine Bundles. Note how these dolls combine buckskin parts with cloth. (MPI) Boys were given dolls like the one below, with miniature weapons, instruments, Horse gear and Bundles. (Heye)

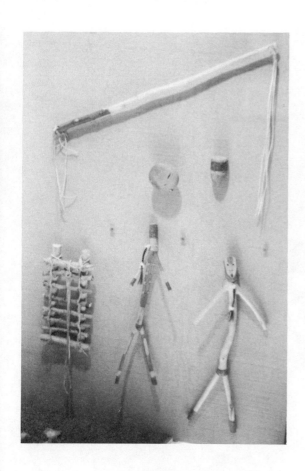

ABOVE LEFT: A display of stick dolls, a small sled, and a whip for spinning two tops, one of wood and the other of stone. ABOVE: A display of two girls' dresses and some toys, including a Painted Lodge, stick Horse and travois, dolls with implements, and a fully-beaded cradle board. BELOW: A close-up of the whip and spinning top, both made from willow. NEXT PAGE: At top is a boy's bow and arrows, made lighter than those for a man. Willow and Birch saplings were common bow woods (for boys), service-berry stems made arrows, and chipped bones made the heads. Below is a sled made from Buffalo ribs fastened with rawhide . (All MPI)

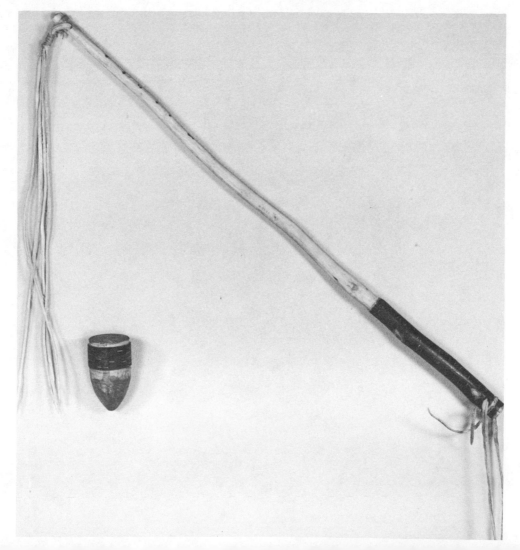

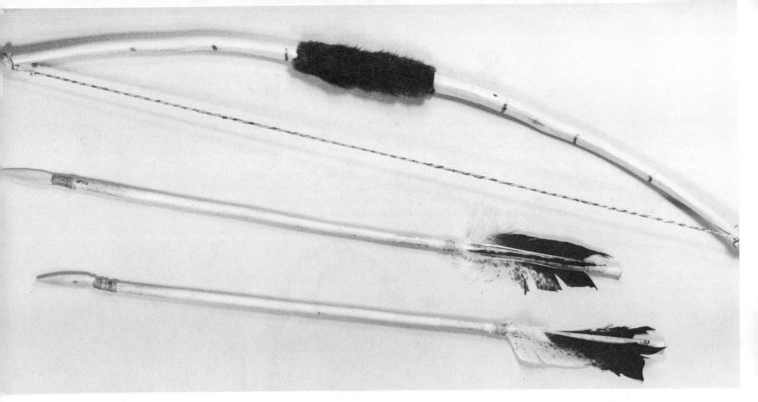

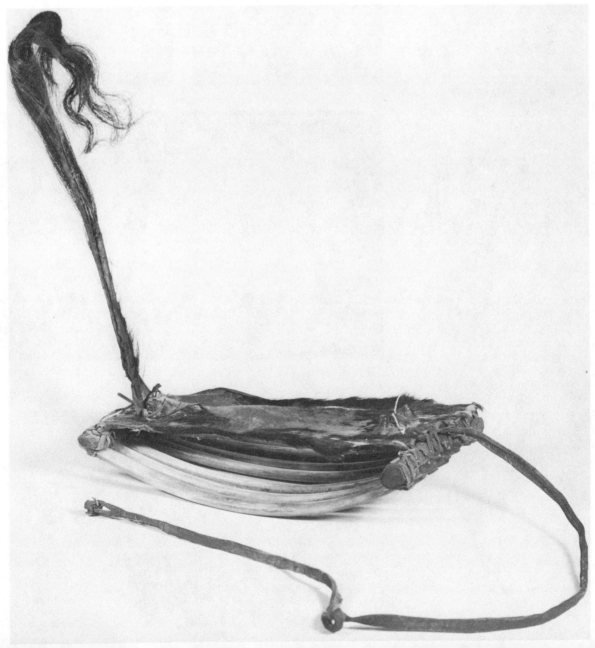

Soft Skin Bags

Soft skin bags were used to hold necklaces, paints, beads, bullets, and other articles of value. Some were made of plain buckskin or fur, some had edgings of beads or quills, and some were fully beaded. Bags for sacred articles were often made from bladders or the whole skins of small Birds and Animals. At left is the skin of a newborn Deer, used as a tobacco pouch. (MPI) At the right is a Buffalo bladder, lined and edged with buckskin and beads, to hold Medicinal herbs. (PMAA) Such materials were dried, scraped, and then rubbed until they got soft. In the center is a small utility pouch, carried by men and women over their shoulders like a purse. (PMAA) Below are two Medicine bags made from Elk's feet, sewn together. (PMAA) At the bottom is a fully-beaded shoulder bag used on hunting and war trips. (Heye)

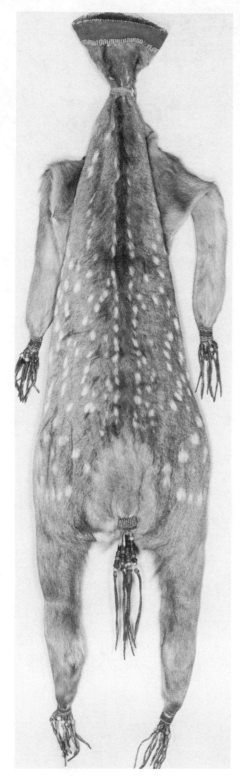

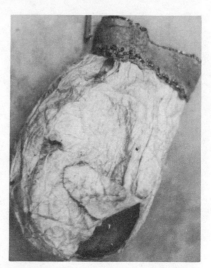

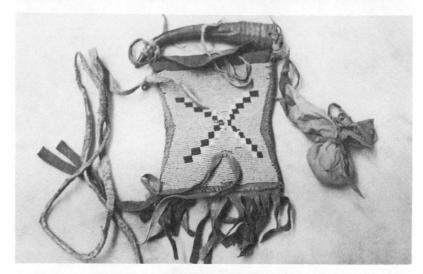

Pipes and Bags

Pipe smoking was so much a part of traditional Blackfoot life that every family had at least one pipe in its possession. Pipes were made by skilled men and women who were paid a riding Horse for a good one. Blackfoot pipes have a distinct appearance, though pipes of other styles were obtained by trade and commonly used. For ceremonial use, however, only the black stone pipes of local make were allowed (and still are).

Blackfoot pipes usually have the appearance of an acorn sitting on a rectangular base. They are made from a hard, grey-colored stone found in several places around the old Blackfoot country. The process begins with the selection of a good stone, which is marked out for the shape of the intended bowl. Holes are then drilled into the stone from two directions, to make an L shape. Hand tools have been used for many years. The drilled stone is then cut to shape with a hacksaw. After this a file is used to make the shape more exact. Final shaping and smoothing is done with sandpaper. To complete the pipe bowl it is worked over a smoky fire to turn it black.

It is said that this common style bowl was inspired by pipes of similar shape used by tribes far to the East, some of whose members came into Blackfoot country with the first trappers and traders. More ancient Blackfoot pipes had straight bowls of tubular shape, often made so as to have male symbolism. However, for the past hundred years or more this style of pipe has only been used with certain Medicine Bundles.

Pipe stems are made of willow, saskatoon, and chokecherry wood. The favorite wood has been ash, which must be obtained in the country to the East. Holes are put through stems with heated wires. Blackfoot stems are most always round, and seldom decorated beyond very smooth polishing. Wrappings of brass wire and Horse hair were sometimes applied. Quilled stems were usually obtained in trade.

Pipes used by women were usually of the same shape as described, only smaller and shorter. For everyday use women sometimes preferred an L-shaped bowl. Black bowls were sometimes inlaid with lead, either for decoration or for repair, but in that case they were not used in ceremonies. Black bowls of other shapes, and with inlays of other colors, were usually obtained from other tribes.

Smoking pipes are kept in pipe bags which are usually of buckskin, though sometimes simply of cloth. Buckskin pipe bags usually have fully beaded panels at their bottoms, sometimes just on one side, other times on both. These are done in the apllique stitch, often with floral patterns. Blackfoot pipe bags have long fringes, sometimes with large beads strung on them, but without the elaborate quillwork decoration used by some other tribes. Sizes of pipe bags vary, though the ones used by women are generally quite smaller.

Most Blackfoot pipes formed part of a smoking kit that included the following: A slender, pointed stick used for tamping; one or more pouches for tobacco--often the foetus of a Deer or some other Animal; matches or, formerly, flint and steel; and a cutting board on which everything was prepared. Cutting boards are about one foot square, usually decorated with brass tacks, and have a hollow in the center for the tobacco. Ceremonial containers for tobacco include the skins of Birds and small Animals, usually with a sack sewn inside their bodies.

elow is a typical man's smoking pipe, with a black bowl and round stem. A large crack has been repaired with lead. (MPI

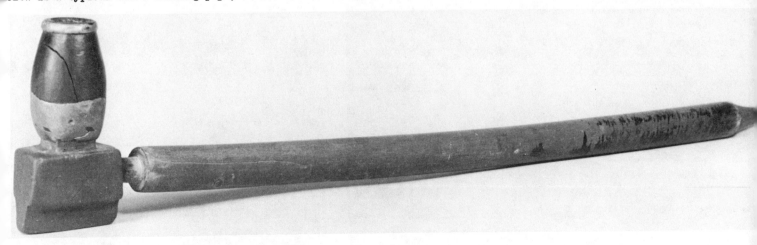

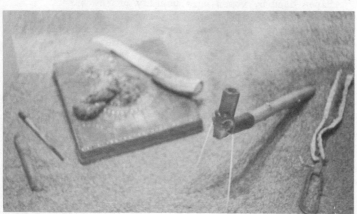

TOP TO BOTTOM: Four Blackfoot pipe bowls, including one of white stone. Next, a smoking kit, including cutting board, knife, twist tobacco, tamping sticks, steel for fire, and a pipe with the carved head of a Mountain Sheep, which probably came by trade. (Both MPI) Next, two pipe bags, along with some small paint bags, pointed awl cases, and a rolled up belt. Then, three bags, with a pipe and tamper. (Both PMAA) Of the two pipe bags below, the one at right is far older. It is decorated with Real Beads and quillwork. (Both from Heye)

NEXT PAGE: Two photos at left show more designs on pipe bags, including one with the flag of Alberta. (Both PMAA) At right are the fronts and backs of three pipe bags. (LM) Below are four women's pipes. (MPI)

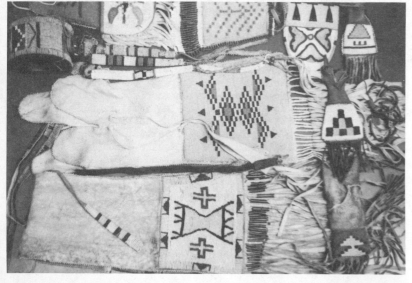

68

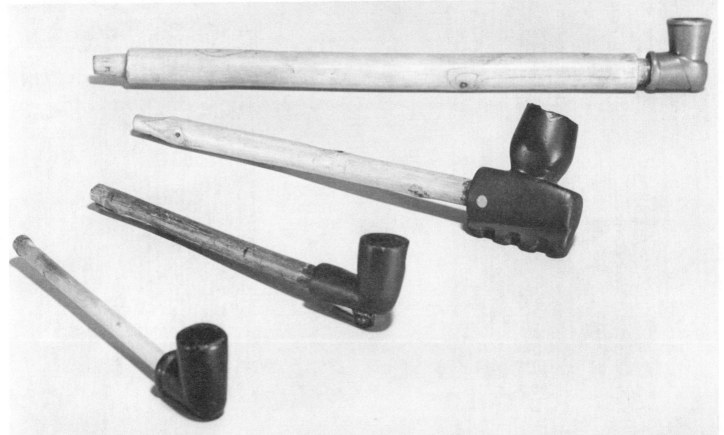

Gun Cases

Common gun cases, in the Old Days, were probably not as fancy as these, but the two in these photos are typical of the style carried by well-dressed men after the Reservation days began. (MPI)

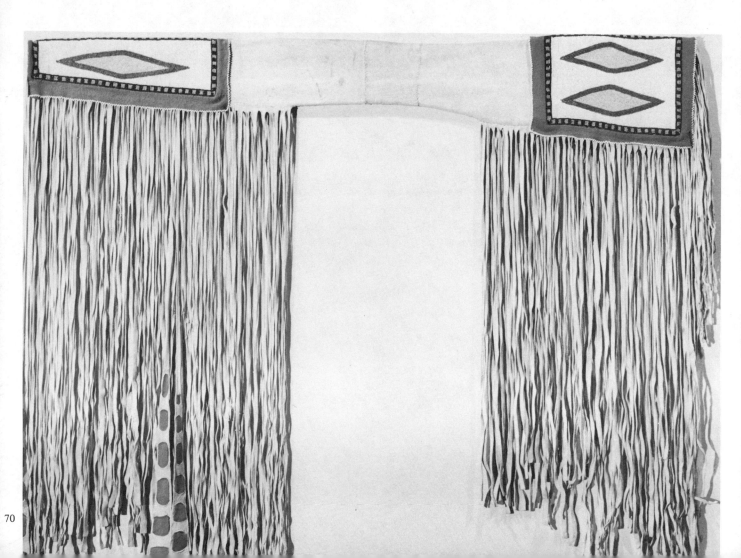

Bows and Arrows

Bows used for hunting and battling were quite strong. They usually had a double curve and were backed with sinew to make them stronger. Bow strings were of sinew, also. Ash was apparently the favorite kind of wood. Good arrows were usually made from branches of Serviceberry or Chokecherry, sometimes of Willow. Variations included points of stone, bone, metal, and wood, and various markings and colorings to identify the owner. Photos, below, show an old, sinew-backed bow (PMAA), a buckskin quiver and bow case (LM), a museum drawer full of arrows, showing variations in points and ends (PMAA), and a drilled Buffalo-rib bone used as an arrow straightener (Heye).

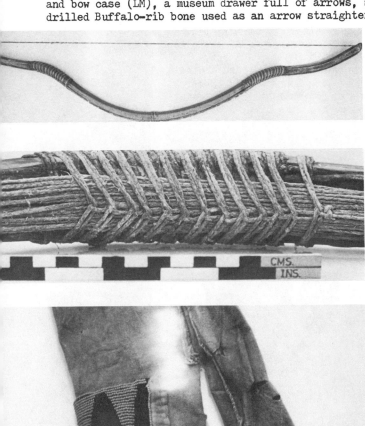

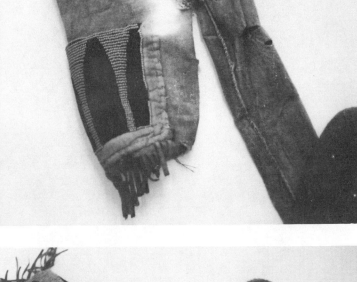

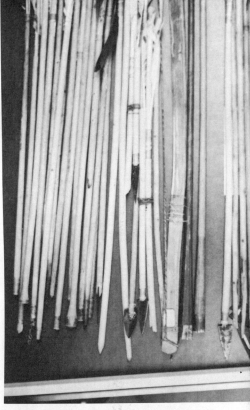

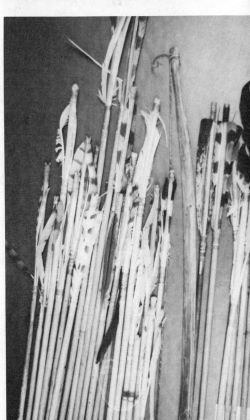

Instruments

In the Old Days all Blackfoot instruments were for ceremonial use, with the possible exception of flutes that were used by some men to court women and entertain the People. The most popular instrument has long been the hand drum, which is made by stretching a wet piece of rawhide over a wooden hoop such as the lid of a cheese box. This hide is laced along the side of the drum and across the back. Below is a large group drum made from a hollowed log. This one was used for the Grass Dance, which was adopted from Eastern tribes in the late 1800's. The drum style may have been adopted, also. (Heye) In the center is a rawhide rattle of the kind used in many ceremonies, such as the Sun Dance and Beaver Bundle. It is made of two pieces of rawhide, sewn together while wet and stuffed with sand to make the shape. The sand is poured out when the rawhide dries, small stones are inserted, and a handle is attached. At right is a whistle made from an Eagle-wing bone. (MPI) Such whistles were used for doctoring, in ceremonies, and in personal Medicines. At the bottom is a rattle used by members of societies, such as the Crazy Dogs. (MPI)

Horse Gear

The two most important articles of Blackfoot Horse gear are the bridle, which was usually of Buffalo skin or braided hair, looped over the lower jaw, and the travois, on which a household's belongings were packed. The photo below shows a travois from the ancient days, when Dogs were used for packing. (Heye) A small photo on the right shows two toy travois of the Dog style. Those used on Horses were about the same, exept larger and with the pole tips extending more in the shape of an X. (AMNH) The smallest photo shows a man's pad saddle of a typical style, made of buckskin and filled with hair. (PMAA) Men and women also used frame saddles made of wood, rawhide, and sometimes Elk horns. Nearly every rider used a quirt, often of Elk horn, like the old one shown below. (Heye) When the People settled on the Reservation and could afford to have articles of luxury they often made very elaborate Horse gear that they used for parades and other special occasions. The photo on the lower right shows typical decorations for such gear, on two cruppers. (PMAA) Other decorated gear included saddles, stirrups, martingales, and various saddle bags. Materials for decorating included large pieces of trade cloth, partial beading, and dangling strings of beads and bells. Geometric designs were applied to some gear in the Old Days.

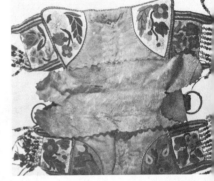

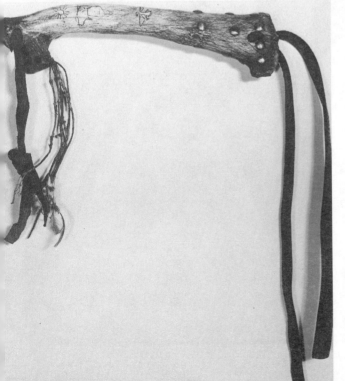

Backrests

Backrests were the main furniture items in traditional Blackfoot households. A Blackfoot "couch" consists of a bed of robes and blankets, with a backrest at the head and another at the foot. Backrests are made of peeled Willows strung together with sinews. The sketch shows how the stringing is done. The frame is tied to six main stakes, while its tension is adjusted by laying weights (like stones) on strings attached to two additional stakes, at the head. The small sketch shows the kind of loop used to tie the Willows to each of the three frame cords. The loops are pulled tight to bring the Willows next to each other. Sometimes they are knotted between each Willow, as well. Older backrests often have two more strings running up through holes in the Willows, to give extra support. The two photos below show the front and back of the same backrest. The buckskin loop goes over a wooden tripod which supports the whole backrest. In front this is covered up by an ornate flap which is usually made of wool, with some beading and fringe. Edging and other decorations are also of wool. (PMAA)

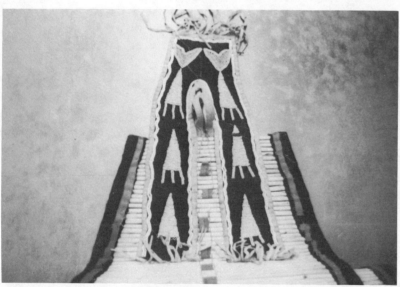

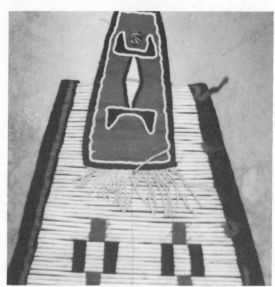

Parfleche

Parfleches served as containers for food and clothing in old-time Blackfoot households. They took the place of suitcases and trunks. Usually they were made in matching pairs, from a fresh cowhide. The hide was staked on the ground, hair-side down, and fleshed. Then the parfleches were marked out and the designs drawn in. Colors were mainly red and green, with some black for outlines and blue or yellow for variation. The rest of the hide was marked out for other rawhide bags and for moccasin soles. The hair was then scraped off, and the articles cut out. The sketch shows a parfleche pattern with lines marking the folds and circles showing the thong holes used for tying the parfleche shut.

(Examples on top from PMAA, bottom from MPI)

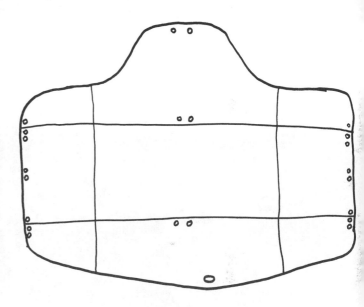

Utensils

The most basic utensil among the Blackfoot People has always been the knife. Though the ancient People made their own, of flint and other stone, metal knives from traders have been in use for two hundred years or more. Another very important utensil, or tool, was the flesher, for taking the meat and fat from hides, and the scraper, for taking the hair off. The upper photo, at left, shows fleshers of bone and steel. All have flattened edges with tooth-like cuts. The lower photo shows scrapers, some of wood and some of Elk horn, all with steel blades fastened on with rawhide thongs. (Both PMAA) The center photos show two eating utensils. Bowls were hollowed out from knots of Ash or Cottonwood. Cups were made from smaller knots. Both were sanded, dried, and greased. Horn spoons were made by first throwing a fresh horn into the fire to clean it out, then carving it with a knife, and finally boiling it to make it soft and pliable.
At that point a stone of the right shape was placed inside the bowl and wrapped up tight with strips of hide. The handle was bent to shape and held in place with weights. The finished spoon was sanded and greased. The handle was often decorated with quillwork, like the one below, which is made from a Cow-horn. (Heye) Old ones were made from the horns of Buffalo and Mountain Sheep.
At the right is an article carried by most People in the Old Days. It is a steel, obtained from traders, for use in fire-making (with flint and punk) and for sharpening knives. This one hung from a woman's belt by the decorated strap. (MPI)

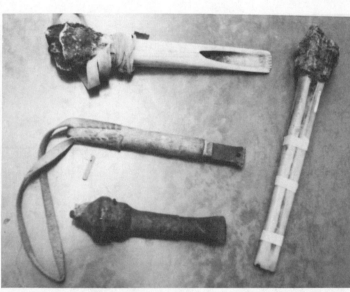

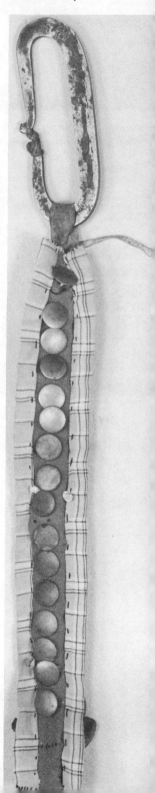

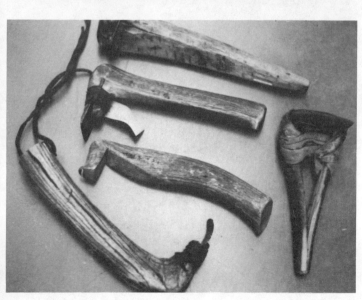

Some Directions

In the next few pages we will describe some of the basic craftwork techniques; this is mainly because many of these books will be used in school class-rooms where young People will be inspired by the photos and will want to know a little about the actual making of similar articles. After reading this book we encourage you to go to your Elders for more personal instructions. Bring them tobacco and presents, and give them your respectful attention. Finally, try to follow their instructions excactly as they give them to you. That is the Blackfoot Way.

BEADS

Because beadwork and the use of beads is the most popular form of craftwork practiced today, we will say a few things about this. Beads made of dried Berries, Fish and Snake vertebrae, claws, teeth, shells, and other natural articles have been used by Blackfoot People for untold generations. Mostly they were strung on necklaces or fastened to the fringes of some article. However, for more than 200 years the most popular beads among the Blackfoot People have been made by bead craftsmen and women in different European countries--especially Italy--and imported to this continent for distribution to the People by traders and other merchants. Virtually every sacred and ceremonial article of Blackfoot origin--among the People, or in museums--has some of these European beads among its decorations.

John Ewers gives a good history of Blackfoot beadwork in his book, Blackfeet Crafts. He says that some trade beads may have reached the Blackfoot People in the early 1700's through trade with tribes who were then in direct contact with merchants. By the 1780's some of these merchants had made their way directly to the Blackfoot People. By the 1830's many important men and women in the tribe already wore shirts and dresses decorated with large embroidery beads known today as "pony beads." Sky blue and white were the most common color combinations. This early beadwork generally followed the styles and designs of quillwork. Many articles were then decorated with a combination of quills and beads.

The Old People called these early beads "real beads." By 1870 eight hanks of these beads were valued at one good Buffalo robe. A hank had about ten 8-inch strings of beads. The larger "necklace beads" were much more valuable. Some old strings of them are still passed on as family heirlooms. Many styles of necklace beads have been used. Among the most prized, and longest in use, are those known as "Skunk beads." They are fairly large, usually of blue glass, with raised, hand-painted designs of small, red and white flower buds, connected by vine-like lines. Some are left today, in Medicine Bundles.

The type of beads and style of beadwork most common today is said to have become popular among the Blackfoot People during the 1870's. Seed beads were then introduced in such small sizes (mostly less than half that of the "real beads") that Blackfoot women began to show their artistic skills with beadwork of intricate patterns and many colors. Many articles that had, before, been mostly decorated with borders or individual designs were now fully-covered with beads. Beaded designs of leaves and colorful flowers became very popular.

BEADWORKING

Most Blackfoot beadwork is characterized by certain color and design combinations, along with the use of a technique known as "applique" or "overlay" stitch. With this method two strings are used to make one row of beadwork. The beads are strung on one string and sewn down with another, which is regularly crossed over the other. This generally makes all the beads lie firm and close to the material the article is made out of. This style contrasts with that used by many other tribes on the Plains--the "lazy stitch"--in which the beads are sewn down, a few at a time, with the same thread they are strung on. This produces ridge-shaped rows of beadwork in which the beads are often somewhat loose.

THE OVERLAY STITCH
Side view and top view

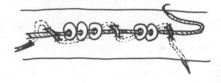

Popular colors used by traditional Blackfoot bead-workers include light and dark blue, "greasy" yellow, "Cheyenne" pink, rose, and dark green. Of course many other colors were used, as well, in a great variety of shades. The old-time seed beads were made in Italy, and are known as "Italian beads" by merchants. They are of good glass, and the colors are very soft and subtle. They are of uneven shapes which gives the finished beadwork a special texture. Most modern beads are sold as "Czechoslovakian beads," since that's where they are made. They have pretty even shapes and very bright colors.

Blackfoot geometric beadwork designs are often large figures made up by carefully combining many smaller ones, usually beginning with squares, stripes, triangles, or rectangles. Each minor design within a large design is usually a different color. A few designs have common names, such as the "mountain design" and "feather design." Otherwise, however, there are no tribal meanings to any beaded designs--only what each beadworker might think on her own.

SEWING

We have seen many nice craft articles, especiallly in recent years, that were spoiled because of poor sewing. Fully beaded moccasins sewn with weak thread so that many of the beads were fallen off, or a buckskin suit spoiled by careless stitches and crooked seams. In the drawings below are the four main stitches used for traditional Blackfoot sewing. For the sake of appearance it is important to make neat and even stitches. For durability it is important to catch two pieces with a deep-enough stitch that won't tear through, yet not so deep that the sinew or thread is exposed to wear. This often happens on moccasin soles, where an exposed stitch soon wears out.

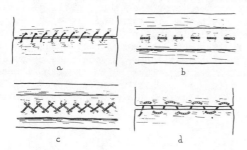

Stitch A is used on moccasin soles and other seams. Articles sewn with this stitch are generally turned inside out when finished. This is the "over and over" stitch. Stitch B is the "running" stitch, which is used to attach borders and bands to a main piece. In the making of rawhide bags, for instance, a buckskin thong follows this stitch in holding down a strip of red wool along the edges of the bags. Stitch C is used mainly for mending. Stitch D is used when needed for its pleasing appearance, as in the exposed seams of buckskin shirts and dresses.

The ancient thread of the Blackfoot People is sinew, which is still used for some craftwork. It comes in shiny strips from along the back and legs of Animals like Buffalo, Elk, Deer, or Cattle. The wet strips are scraped clean with a knife, then plastered on a tipi pole and left to dry. It can then be pulled apart into many narrow or wide strands as needed for sewing and wrapping. Before using the strand it is softened by soaking--in the mouth or in water--and then twisted by holding one end and rolling the rest between two palms or across a lap. In the Old Days one point of the strand was left dry and stiff so that it could be poked through small sewing holes made with sharp, pointed awls of bone. Some People still follow this process for sewing seams, using a metal-tipped awl instead of bone. But those who do beadwork with sinew usually string it on a needle. Needles and commercial thread have been available to the People since the early traders came. Even sewing machines were common by the turn-of-the-century, especially for sewing articles of cloth.

HIDE TANNING

In the Old Days every Blackfoot woman was able to tan the hides of Animals shot by the family's hunters. The tanning processes that they used were simple to learn, but very difficult to keep up as actual work. Girls learned to help the women, early. Especially good tanners were always noted by the People.

The tanning of a Buffalo hide began with the chore of removing the fat and meat from the flesh side of a fresh hide. For this work the hide was staked out on the ground, hair-side down, with a couple dozen stakes driven through the edges so that the hide was tight. A chisel-like fleshing tool was used with chopping movements. The hide was then left for a few days to dry out and bleach. After this the flesh side was evened out with a scraper.

The scraper was again used, after the hide was turned over and staked down, to remove all the hair, if the hide was being made into leather instead of a robe. With the flesh side dry and even, and the hair side looking about the same, the hide was properly a "rawhide." As such, it could be cut up and made into parfleches, moccasin soles, ropes, and so on.

To continue tanning a rawhide it was rubbed with a mixture of brains, fat, and liver saved from the Animal. Lard, flour, and warm water were used as a mixture in later years. This mixture was rubbed thoroughly into the hide with the hands and with a smooth stone. The hide was then left to dry some more. When dry, it was soaked in warm water until it could be rolled into a tight bundle.

Next, the now-shrunken hide was stretched and worked back into shape with the feet and hands. Then, as it slowly dried, it was continuously rubbed and stretched to break down the tissues and make it soft. A loop of thick, twisted rawhide was tied, like a bow-string, to the under side of an inclined lodge pole. The rolled up hide was sawed back and forth through this loop. A dull scythe blade has been used for this purpose in more recent times. The friction from rubbing the hide creates heat which dries it and makes it softer.

Tanned hides for everyday use were generally smoked after tanning. For this, a fire was built into coals, then covered with rotten wood. Different trees give different shades from smoking. The hide was sewn shut into a pointed tipi shape, with an opening at the bottom. It was then suspended over the smoking wood and held down at the sides so that the smoke had a hard time getting out. It did not take long to smoke the hide thoroughly.

PAINTING

Long, long before colorful beadwork became the style among the Blackfoot People craftworkers had ways of artistry for adding color to their creations. Since most articles were then made of hide, this coloring work became known as hide painting. Examples of this kind of work can be seen today on the outsides of the sacred Painted Lodges, and on the rawhide bags that contain many of the remaining Medicines.

Different colored earths were most used for hide painting. White, black, and various shades of red and yellow were obtained in this way. Green paint came from a certain kind of mud. Blue was made by drying certain kinds of Duck manure. Some artists were good at mixing colors. Since the same paints were also used for ceremonial purposes, their gathering and use was respected as sacred. Certain kinds of Red Paint, especially, have often been applied to articles only in ceremonial ways. Paints are also valued as traditional articles of trade.

Natural paints were dried, ground to powder, and kept in small buckskin "paint bags." The method by which an article was painted depended on its planned use. For many articles the powdered paint was simply mixed with some hot water, often in a clam shell cup or a tin cup. If the painting was due to much wear, the powders were often mixed with a glue-like substance made by boiling in water the tail of a Beaver or the inner scrapings of a hide. For lodge paintings the colors were often mixed with hot broth. In later years there have been many substitutes for natural paints, including crayons, poster paints, colored pencils, and household latex paints. All of these work well, though some look very modern and none have the traditional sacred feeling.

"Paint brushes" were made in several ways. Most common were those made from the porous parts of Animal shoulder blades or hip bones. They were cut in a shape similar to the front half of a tongue. The front part was either rounded for painting large areas, or pointed for making fine lines and edges. The pores held the liquid paint until it was brushed on an article. Good artists took care of their many brushes, bags of paint, shells, and so on. They were regularly hired by those not so artistic.

Both men and women did hide painting. Most articles with geometric designs were painted by women, while sacred symbols and picture-stories of brave exploits were usually painted by men.

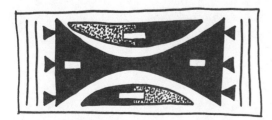

QUILLWORK

An ancient Blackfoot art for decorating clothing and other articles of soft hide is that of sewing down the quills of a Porcupine so that they form patterns and designs. The art of Quillwork was first taught to the long-ago People by Thunder. It has, ever since, been regarded as a sacred craft. Those who wish to learn it and practice it go to an experienced Elder to be initiated and instructed. There are yet several People who have been so initiated.

Porcupine quills were used in their natural shades as well as dyed. All the main colors for dyeing were obtained from different Plants, which were usually moistened, covered with quills, and then wrapped up until dry. By that time the color is usually soaked into the quills. When colored cloth was first introduced, by the 1800's, some People dyed their quills by boiling them with the cloth. Others used commercial dyes, in more recent times.

Quillworkers soak the quills in their mouths to soften them, before they are sewed down. Among the basic supplies needed, in addition to quills of various sizes and colors (all kept in separate pouches), are many strands of rolled sinew, an awl, an instrument for flateening down the quills after they are sewed on, and a piece of hide on which to do the work.

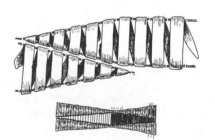

A common method of sewing quills down on buckskin is shown in the drawings above. Two parallel sinew threads are stitched down after each crossing of a quill which is folded back and forth, beginning with the butt end and ending with the tip. The tip and the next butt end are then overlapped in such a way that the joint will not show on the completed work. The width of a quilled band produced in this way is very narrow. Large areas are covered with many of these bands, side by side. The same method is also used to produce shapes of quillwork, as in the last of the drawings above. The patterns are varied by bringing the two threads closer together or further apart.

Bibliography

BLACKFEET CRAFTS, by John C. Ewers. Bureau of Indian Affairs; Haskell Institute, Lawrence, Kansas, 1962.

Blackfeet Women's Clothing, by Richard Conn. AMERICAN INDIAN TRADITION, Alton, Illinois, 1961.

Material Culture of the Blackfoot Indians, by Clark Wissler. ANTHROPOLOGICAL PAPERS OF THE AMERICAN MUSEUM OF NATURAL HISTORY, Vol. 5, pt. 1, New York, 1910.

The fine pen and ink drawings in this book are copied from the last named journal.